Show Boards

Show Boards

Next-Level Platters & Boards That Win the Party

Lea Dixon, The Platter Girl

CASTLE POINT BOOKS

NEW YORK

SHOW BOARDS.
Copyright © 2024 by St. Martin's Press.
All rights reserved. Printed in China. For information,
address St. Martin's Press, 120 Broadway, New York, NY 10271.

www.castlepointbooks.com

The Castle Point Books trademark is owned by Castle Point Publishing, LLC.
Castle Point books are published and distributed by St. Martin's Publishing Group.

ISBN 978-1-250-33978-2 (paper over board)
ISBN 978-1-250-33979-9 (ebook)

Design by Melissa Gerber
Photography by Lea Dixon except photo on page 9 courtesy of Emily Zamora/Simply Wandering Photography
and photos on pages 33, 74, 90, 102, 107, 114, and 129 used under license from Shutterstock.com

Edited by Jennifer Leight
Special thanks to Keeley Nichols

Our books may be purchased in bulk for promotional, educational, or business use.
Please contact your local bookseller or the Macmillan Corporate and Premium Sales Department
at 1-800-221-7945, extension 5442, or by email at MacmillanSpecialMarkets@macmillan.com.

First Edition: 2024

10 9 8 7 6 5 4 3 2 1

To my family and friends for putting up
with my shenanigans and always eating
my crazy food creations

Contents

WELCOME TO THE SHOW **8**

GET THE PARTY STARTED **11**

FRESH TAKES ON FRUITS & FLORALS **19**

HOME & HEART **37**

THE GREAT OUTDOORS **55**

SPRING & SUMMER CELEBRATIONS **69**

FALL & WINTER WONDERS **87**

CHARCUTERIE CHARACTERS **119**

CREATIVE STATEMENTS ANYTIME **137**

INDEX **154**

Welcome to the *Show*

No more basic boards. Congratulations, you are about to become an avant-garde charcuterie artist and host of the year! Your canvas is a platter or a board, and your opening night is your next entertaining event. All you need to get started making edible masterpieces that will wow your guests—from fields of flowers and the night sky to adorable creatures and custom houses—is in this book.

It's an unbelievable feeling to surprise and delight friends and family with spectacular, eye-catching displays of party food. Perhaps even more amazing is how simple it can be to craft showstopping spreads that taste as good as they look. You can easily elevate any celebration with the fifty creative designs and tons of artful tips in the pages that follow.

Surprise your guests with a sea of imaginative platters—from savory Shark-Cuterie (page 83) to whipped honey butter waves of the Butter Surfboard (page 78). Turn up the fun with an edible Boom Box Board straight out of the '80s (page 138). Show your love and gather smiles with fun carved fruits (pages 51, 129, and 151). Create a clever grill out of a watermelon and serve with fruit steaks and skewers (page 77). Even give the gift of holiday peace by centering the Thanksgiving conversation safely on the great grazing displays—something everyone can agree on (pages 94, 98, 102, and 107)! That's just a sampling of the boards (and inspiration for your own designs) you'll discover.

Whatever you choose, you'll find it incredibly rewarding to make a statement piece that brings everyone around the table. Every creation can be a reminder that food is a way to come together and celebrate our connection. In fact, if you're open to sharing the spotlight, invite friends and family (especially the kids in your life) in on the charcuterie-construction fun.

So get ready to bring more energy, creativity, and joy to all of your gatherings! You'll show your guests love and make lasting memories as you accept your party-host crown.

XOXO, Lea

Get the Party Started

Food can be a big part of the magic in events we host for friends and family. Yet it often becomes simply a to-do we check off a list before we jump into decorations. Why do we resort to putting out the same old party trays when we could offer standout charcuterie boards that help our guests feel appreciated and make us look like the star of a kitchen competition show? *Show Boards* is here to inspire you; you don't need to settle for fine! This book is just what you need to treat yourself and your guests to food as part of the décor— flavorful fun in the form of charcuterie-board art.

It's easy to get started. Any of the boards in this book will bring the wow factor, creating novelty and excitement for the food you serve at your party. The displays will draw people in, start conversations, and allow them to indulge and enjoy. It's a party, and the food table should feel like one! You can customize your creations to celebrate the guest of honor (consider Frappe Fun for your favorite coffee lover on page 148), a certain occasion (Welcome Home on page 38 is perfect for a housewarming), or just the vibe of your guests (All Hands on Board on page 101 brings a spooky aesthetic). You have so many ideas to choose from, along with tips throughout to help you customize your boards!

While your guests marvel at the thoughtfulness shown in your customized edible art, you can simply be present in the moment and savor your role as a magnificent host. Boards save time by making it super-easy to prep ahead.

Even the most elaborate boards can be broken down into steps; many include dip making and produce slicing that can be done the day before. So you can put a picture-perfect spread on the serving table and then step back and enjoy the gathering.

Creative platter concepts are a gift—of course, at your event but also to you as you put them together. Letting your imagination run wild and engaging in a hands-on activity like charcuterie artistry are both amazing ways to relieve stress. You'll get lost in a world of whimsical food creations as you think ahead to your guests' pleased reactions. Soon you'll master the board designs in *Show Boards* and begin branching out with ideas all your own. There is no limit on creativity when you're sharing love, laughter, and food. So let's get the plans started.

MAKE A PLAN

Okay, so you're inspired to throw a party? Getting everything organized is an essential step to hosting a great event. Preparing will make the process more enjoyable for you as well. These are the three big questions to start the party planning and lead you to selecting the perfect board for the occasion:

- What are you celebrating?
- When and where are you going to throw the party?
- Who are you going to invite?

Choosing something to celebrate is the fun part.
Any day can be a charcuterie celebration in my book! But you will probably choose a different board for a kids' birthday party versus a fiftieth-anniversary celebration versus a Thanksgiving gathering. Build your board around the theme using ingredients, colors, and decor to show your guests exactly what they are celebrating.

Select the time and place for the party with guests' comfort and enjoyment and your sanity in mind. Is there enough seating? Is there space to move around comfortably? Is the party going to take place inside or outside—or both? Is there shade? Keep in mind the setting as you choose the board you want to create—and whatever you will need to protect the food from any challenging conditions (think: heat, sand, insects).

Setting the guest list helps you determine how much food to provide and any special needs to consider—such as for kid tastes or food intolerances and allergies. Not sure what needs you should cover? Include a line on the invitation asking your guests to reach out to you about them.

The best-planned events also set your guests' expectations and answer their questions. So be sure to include on the invitations (beyond the basic when and where) whether guests should dress a certain way, bring a present or food, park (or not park) in a certain place, and let themselves in or head to the backyard. Added details can help alleviate any potentially awkward situations or guest anxieties. Just as your platters and boards can make your guests feel welcome, so can covering this kind of information.

MAKE A BOARD

Within the pages of this book, you have fifty fun boards to choose from. But your party-serving options are many more. Try using two or three boards in combination, or upsize servings and designs to make a full grazing table if you are feeding a crowd of twenty or more guests. You can also feature one table with a grazing board display in any size as a centerpiece or surprise element and then add more traditional food offerings off to the side or in another area.

Even within the ideas in this book, you can easily swap in or out ingredients to suit availability, budget, and guest needs and tastes. For best results, seek out local, seasonal foods with vibrant colors and flavors and keep shape and texture in mind so you can create a well-balanced board that sticks with your theme.

The same goes for the boards and platters that are the foundations of your creations. The options used in the board-building instructions and shown in the photos throughout this book work beautifully, but you can find amazing options that work just as well. Keep size and overall aesthetic in mind as you make any substitutions. If you can, have a variety of boards, trays, platters, and pretty plates on hand for building. (Lately, I'm loving olive woods, black walnut, and marble plates.) Try styling dark wood versus light wood, marble versus slate, and trays with edges versus boards without borders. There are a bazillion shapes of platters and boards out there, so have fun and experiment. A round or square shape is an easy place to begin your journey.

With your board and ingredients ready to party, you can begin to bring everything together:

- Wash and dry the produce.

- Unwrap all the cheeses and meats.

- Slice the cheeses.

- Fold the meats.

- Slice the fruits and veggies.

- Add dips, olives, and pickles to bowls.

- Prepare your platter with parchment (as needed to make food-safe).

Because placing lots of ingredients can seem overwhelming at first, I like to use what I call the Eat Beautifully method. It's a simple five-step process that helps me stack my ingredients so the end result is gorgeous every time. It works best with traditional cheese boards and charcuterie-type platters, so give yourself some flexibility when working with a zanier spread of ingredients or presentation.

To follow the Eat Beautifully method, place your prepped ingredients on your platter in this order to achieve a pretty, balanced look:

1. Cheeses & dishes

2. Meats

3. Fruits & veggies

4. Pantry items

5. Garnishes

Then stand back, take a pic, and get ready to party!

1. Cheeses & Dishes

Place your cheeses and dishes on your board, leaving space in between for other ingredients. Aim to include an array of three to five cheeses varying among hard, soft, cow's milk, sheep's milk, and goat's milk cheeses. (I love a six-month sheep's milk Manchego, dill Havarti, aged Gouda, and blueberry-vanilla goat cheese for a beginner grazing board.) Fill two or three small bowls or ramekins with flavorful dips and accents like hummus and pickles or olives. Add in little jars of herbal-infused honey and local fruit spreads for a sweet touch.

Complete the Board Party

To be party-ready, boards benefit from a few buddies.

Parchment paper. Keep it on hand to protect your boards and prep decorative trays.

Ramekins and bowls. Dishes of different sizes welcome many types of ingredients, including jams, pickles, olives, dips, and spreads.

Spoons. Size matters when it comes to spoons. I love to use kiddie spoons to get the best swirl on my dips! Visit yard sales and antique shows to find pretty little spoons for swirling and serving.

Cheese knives. These are super important for digging into your cheeses, so you'll need a variety of knives or cheese forks to add to your collection. Because mixing knives is sort of a no-no when it comes to cheeses, pick up a pack of knives with a variety of styles for each cheese type.

Tongs and other serving tools. Provide little tongs and serving utensils for your guests to grab and serve themselves from your board.

Food labels. It's nice (sometimes essential) to know what type of food you are about to enjoy. Labels come in tons of styles to choose from, including granite and chalkboard varieties or simply skewers with a little paper flag you can write on.

Small plates and napkins. In all the entertaining excitement, don't forget to place these basics next to your graze.

2. Meats

Style your cured meats such as Italian dry salami, dry coppa, and soppressata into roses or tulips, or fold slices into quarters and then slide them onto skewers. Try rolling some plant-based "meats" or piling your board high with smoked salmon. Slice salami chub into thin disks, then stack them into piles on your board. Whatever you choose and however you choose to present it, aim to place the meats next to their complementary cheese pairings.

3. Fruits & Veggies

Colorful fruits and vegetables can really make a board a showstopper! Highlight each piece's natural beauty by presenting it in a beautiful way—whether that's whole, halved, quartered, thinly sliced, or cut in a creative way. You can make fruit look extra fancy with a few simple techniques.

To cut guava and kiwi beautifully, carve in a zigzag fashion around the fruit, making sure to cut to the center. Then gently pull the halves apart.

To score a mango, hold the fruit with the stem pointing up. Cut around the seed, just off-center on both sides to create two "halves." Using a paring knife, cut through the fruit down to the rind but not all the way through to create small squares in the mango flesh. From the rind side, pop the mango flesh outward to show off your creation.

To cut apples and pears into hearts, cut around the core to create two flat halves. Lay each half flat side down and slice it vertically as thinly as you can. Avoiding the center slice, push the slices on both sides up from the bottom to create a heart shape.

To cut strawberries into hearts, simply slice off the tops in a V-shape.

You can find lots of online videos that show creative slicing steps in action. When getting everything on the board in any shape or form, start with larger produce. Then layer in smaller selections like blueberries, grape tomatoes, and cucumber slices.

Pick the Best Produce

A simple guide is to remember the easy acronym CAT, which stands for Color, Appearance, and Texture.

Color: Fruits and vegetables naturally range in color corresponding to their ripeness. When it comes to fruits, typically the more green or less vibrant in outer skin color, the less ripe it is. The brighter or more intense the color, the more ripe it is.

Appearance: Are there any major discolorations, dents, cuts, or wounds on the outer flesh? Avoid any produce with broken skin. When it comes to styling boards, you want to choose the prettiest. Save the misfits for enjoying on the side.

Texture: Give a fruit a little squeeze with your whole hand rather than just a couple of fingers. This will give you a better picture of the overall texture.

4. Pantry Items

It's now time to place all the snacks and dried goods, like nuts, crackers, and dried fruit, but also pretty cookies, fun gummy candies, and chocolate. Have fun matching your pantry items to the color scheme or theme—get creative. Nuts are great for filling in little gaps, and colorful dried fruits can really jazz up a bunch of white cheeses. When you can, include specialty items from local shops—and put some extras in a favor bag for each guest to take home.

5. Garnishes

Garnish with fragrant herbs and nontoxic or edible flowers. Ensuring no pesticides or other harmful chemicals are passed onto your platters is key, so check with the florist or gardener about the right choices for serving with food. Or grow your own gorgeous garnishes. My favorite herbs to garnish with are basil, rosemary, thyme, and sage. My favorite flowers to use are chamomile, carnations, geraniums, and chrysanthemums. Sometimes daisies and roses call out to me too. Lay your fresh garnishes on top of spreads and cheeses, tuck in between ingredients, or delicately drop them on the board. I am telling you, a board can go from blah to wow in .06 second by popping on some pretty touches.

The Platter Playlist

Don't forget music to set the mood! Have fun creating a party playlist that you ingeniously curate prior to your guests' arrival. Or hop onto your favorite streaming music provider five seconds before guests arrive and choose a premade playlist. (Don't worry, I promise I won't judge you!) Or go ahead and delegate a few weeks before the event—a guest will be honored that you value their taste. Music can put people at ease and key into the theme of the party as soon as guests set foot through the door.

MAKE SOME MAGIC

Here are a few more pointers that might just be the trick to helping you absolutely nail your next party board—whether you use the boards in this book as your inspiration or dream up a brand-new showstopping board.

Shop fresh and local. Go for organic ingredients as often as you can. Choose brightly colored produce that pairs nicely with your cheese and dip selections. (I think of the rainbow when I shop for produce.) Keep texture and height in mind as you style your ingredients to create visual interest and draw oohs and aahs from your crowd.

Paint with color. Adding color is my favorite part of designing a board. I like to think of the ingredients as my art medium that I can use to paint my beautiful masterpiece. When it comes to colorful ingredients, we can't help but think of using fruits and vegetables. But don't forget about vibrant dried fruits like apricots, cranberries, and even strawberries. Try adding brightly colored pastries, cookies, and fun candies or chocolates. Use colorful decorations, brightly colored flowers, and on-theme elements to enhance your creation.

Never skimp on cheese or half fill dishes. The cheese and dishes are the foundation for your board and you will arrange other ingredients around them. If you don't have enough cheeses to span the board, you won't have balance—and it will show. And when you add dip to a bowl or olives to a ramekin, fill it up. Leave no more than ¼ to ½ inch of space at the top of your bowls and ramekins. Your guests want to feel lavished. Make sure to garnish the tops as these are one of the first things people see when approaching a board or table.

Feature ingredients you and your guests actually like, not just what you *think* should be included on a board. Let's be honest, you like chocolate. I like chocolate. Why not make things simple and just add some? Treat guests to yogurt-covered pretzels in fun colors or adorable custom cookies.

At the same time, don't be afraid to try something new and invite your guests to do the same. Go wild with tasty nuts like dill pickle almonds, Thai curry cashews, or sweet and spicy pecans. Add some wasabi peas—they are such a gorgeous color!

Set a realistic timeline. Making boards can take longer than you might think to get the details right, so give yourself plenty of time between purchasing your groceries and setting your board down on the table at the party.

Give yourself plenty of grace. You'll want to carefully plan and prepare as much as possible so your guests can have a fantastic experience. But always remember that it's a party. Everyone—including you—is supposed to have fun! It will be okay if things don't go as planned; stay flexible and know there is always a solution.

Bottom line: Celebrations and charcuterie are meant for sharing. The magic is in delicious food that shows appreciation for your guests and is prepared by you with love. I hope the showstopping boards and creative tips in the following pages can add enchantment and a memorable touch to all your fantastic parties. Each platter you make is like a work of art from the heart dedicated to those you care about. What will you create?

Show Me Your Show Board

I want to see your insanely gorgeous creations via social media. Share them with me on Instagram or TikTok @the_platter_girl. Include the occasion, special ingredients or features, and the rave reviews.

Fresh Takes on Fruits & Florals

Blooming Basket	20
Pineapple Perfection	23
Sunflower Spread	24
Peachy Picnic	27
Wildflower Crudités	28
Taco Flower Power	31
Edible Vase	35

Blooming Basket

SERVES 4–6

USES 16" SQUARE BOARD + DRESSING CUPS AND SMALL FLOWER COOKIE CUTTER

No green thumb or expert kitchen skills are required to create this botanical beauty. All you need is a board and a plan. Delicate slices of salami, cleverly carved citrus fruits, and artfully arranged berries and grapes become flower petals. Luscious cheeses form the basket. If your guest list grows, upsize your board and basket and let edible blooms spread even farther.

6 ounces creamy Havarti

1 (2-ounce) Manchego with rind

24 slices Italian dry salami

6 strawberries, hulled and thinly and vertically sliced

10–12 blackberries

3 clementines

1 lemon

1 lime

4 small bunches red grapes

16–18 blueberries

½ English cucumber, sliced into disks and halved (about 28 half circles)

10 fresh oregano sprigs

1. Using the cookie cutter, cut a portion of the Harvarti into 8 to 10 flowers; set aside. Slice the remaining Havarti into 32 to 34 thin rectangles. Starting about halfway down the board, place three slightly overlapping rectangles in each of eight horizontal rows. To create the tapered basket shape, overlap the rectangles slightly more with each row or choose smaller rectangles to use on lower rows. Outline the bottom and sides of the basket and fill in any gaps with the remaining Harvarti.

2. Slice the Manchego into three long thin rectangles. To create the top border of the basket, place the Manchego rectangles horizontally, with the rind facing up.

3. To make a salami rose, place 12 slices of salami in a row, overlapping each at the midpoint. Roll the slices tightly into a bundle and secure in a dressing cup. Make any adjustments to resemble a rose. Repeat to create a second salami rose. Place the roses on the board.

4. To make a strawberry rose, arrange half of the slices around the edge of a dressing cup. Place a blackberry in the center. Repeat to create a second strawberry rose. Place the roses on the board.

5. To create the clementine, lemon, and lime flowers, carve in a zigzag fashion around each fruit, making sure to cut to the center. Then gently pull the halves apart and arrange on the board.

6. Place the Havarti flowers and grapes on the board.

7. Fill in the gaps with the blueberries and the remaining blackberries.

8. Tuck a few cucumber slices and the oregano sprigs around the flowers to look like greenery. Place the remaining cucumber slices in an overlapping pattern as a bottom border for the board.

Pineapple Perfection

This pineapple imposter is a creamy cheese ball in disguise! Your guests will enjoy the added surprise of juicy peach and pineapple pieces when they dig in. Baguette slices make great bite-size bases for the tangy cheese and fruit mixture. (Add more on the side if you're expecting a crowd.) Top with pecans and berries, then add a drizzle of honey for a truly delightful flavor combination. For extra fun, pair with Watermelon Barbecue (page 77).

16 ounces cream cheese, softened to room temperature

8 ounces goat cheese, softened to room temperature

¼ cup pineapple juice

2 tablespoons honey + additional for serving (optional)

1 teaspoon garlic powder

1 teaspoon onion powder

1 teaspoon sea salt

1 teaspoon freshly ground black pepper

½ cup chopped fresh pineapple + reserved crown

1 peach, diced

¾–1 cup pecan halves

French baguette, cut into 12 slices

12 ounces blueberries

1. To prepare the pineapple cheese ball: In a food processor, combine the cream cheese, goat cheese, pineapple juice, honey, garlic powder, onion powder, salt, and pepper until smooth. Transfer to a mixing bowl.

2. Stir the pineapple and peach into the cheese mixture until well combined.

3. Form the mixture into a ball, then flatten slightly into a disk. Refrigerate until just before serving.

4. After removing the mixture from the refrigerator, place it on parchment paper or a food-safe platter. Shape it into an oval to form the pineapple. Gently insert the flat end of the pineapple crown into one end of the cheese oval.

5. Place the pecans on the cheese oval, starting near the crown and moving along in rows to resemble pineapple rind. Cover the sides as well.

6. To assemble the rest of the platter, add the baguette slices (warmed, if desired) at the base of the platter. Fill in the rest of the board with the blueberries. Serve with additional honey on the side (if using).

Details, details . . .

You can split pecans to fill in little gaps and more completely cover the cheese. It's your choice how detail-oriented you get.

Sunflower Spread

Share the joy of a bold sunflower anytime! It's flower arranging made easy: form the petals with slices of Gouda, sweet apricots, and juicy peaches. The middle is made with plump raisins and a scattering of olives. The stalks and leaves of the sunflower are crisp celery sticks and cucumbers with sprigs of fresh parsley. Add honey and dip accents, and done. The whimsical display will look stunning on your table.

6 ounces red-wax Gouda, wax removed, sliced into 14 triangles

½ cup raisins

18 Castelvetrano olives, patted dry

2 or 3 peaches, thinly cut into 24 slices

26 dried apricots

6–8 celery sticks

4 or 5 Persian cucumbers, sliced

8 fresh curly parsley sprigs

2 ounces honey

2 ounces grainy yellow mustard

2 ounces tzatziki

1. Cut the parchment paper to the desired sunflower height. Put the charger plate at the top, then stack the round board on top of that.

2. Place the Gouda slices in a sunburst pattern around the board, allowing the points to extend past the edge of the board by about an inch.

3. Add the raisins to the center of the board, pushing them to the outer rim to make room for the olives.

4. Place the olives to create the center of the flower.

5. Add the peach slices in between the Gouda slices.

6. Place about 10 dried apricots around the edge of the raisins. Line the remainder around the charger plate.

7. Place a few celery sticks in a line, creating the desired stem length and trimming as needed. Create four extra branches.

8. Place the cucumber slices at the end of each celery branch. Add two parsley sprigs to each set of cucumbers to create leaves.

9. Put the honey, mustard, and tzatziki in the ramekins and position them near the branches.

Peachy Picnic

SERVES 8 | USES 16" OVAL BOARD

Serve a pretty picnic on your table! Make this your go-to cheese and fruit ~~platter~~ picnic basket anytime you want to indulge in bright summer flavors and colors. If you haven't tried goat cheese and peaches together, you're in for a tangy-sweet treat. Any fresh garnish can work in place of basil—try edible flowers too.

8 ounces cream cheese, softened to room temperature, divided

6 ounces mango-habanero goat cheese, softened (I recommend Laura Chenel)

1 peach, chopped into small pieces

Honey

Sea salt to taste

6 ounces cranberry-cinnamon goat cheese

¼ cup chopped walnuts

2 teaspoons ground cinnamon

2 peaches, halved or quartered and grilled (see grilling tip below)

3 peaches, thinly sliced

4 clementines, whole

8 ounces Manchego, sliced into triangles

12 strawberries, halved

¼ cup dried cranberries

Fig crackers (I use black fig and poppy seed)

Fresh basil leaves, for garnish

1. In a mixing bowl, combine 4 ounces of the cream cheese with the mango-habanero goat cheese, the chopped peach, a drizzle of honey, and sea salt. Refrigerate the mixture for 10 to 20 minutes.

2. In another bowl, combine the remaining cream cheese with the cranberry-cinnamon goat cheese, chopped walnuts, cinnamon, a drizzle of honey, and sea salt. Refrigerate the mixture for 10 to 20 minutes.

3. After chilling, roll portions of each cheese mixture into bite-size balls. Return to the refrigerator until you are ready to arrange the board.

4. To arrange the board, first place the cheese balls. Add the grilled peaches, sliced peaches, and clementines.

5. Tuck in the Manchego triangles and strawberries. Fill in any gaps with the cranberries.

6. Add about 10 crackers to the top of the board to look like a basket handle. (Serve more on the side.) Garnish with the basil.

Punch up peach flavor by grilling.

For indoor grilling, melt a few tablespoons of butter in a grill pan over medium heat. Add the peaches. As soon as nice grill marks form, remove the peaches from the heat and sprinkle them with cinnamon sugar. Cool and make sure they aren't drippy before adding to the board. Use parchment paper under any wet ingredients or place them in ramekins.

Wildflower Crudités

SERVES 6–8 | USES 24" PADDLE BOARD + 3 RAMEKINS

Brighten any gathering with vibrant vegetable wildflowers! Classic crudités look even more elegant and appealing when you present them in a board scene. Once you've put the creamy hummus and tofu spread into ramekins, don't forget to dress them up. With the back of a spoon, push the surface of the hummus and spread into a swirl shape while holding the bowl secure with your other hand.

2 ounces balsamic hummus

2 ounces jalapeño tofu spread (I like Toby's lite variety)

2 ounces ranch dressing

1 (5-ounce) Boursin Shallot & Chive cheese

20–22 pickled mini sweet peppers

6 ounces precooked black-eyed peas

6 pickled asparagus spears, trimmed to varying lengths

3 pickled carrot spears, trimmed to varying lengths

6 mini sweet peppers, halved

Leaves of 1 green endive

1 head broccoli, cut into florets

18–20 mini heirloom cherry tomatoes

18–20 whole green olives

4–6 stuffed piquanté peppers

4–6 cornichons

2 Babybel cheeses, plastic removed and wax left intact

Fresh Thai basil leaves, for garnish

Edible flowers, for garnish

1. Fill the ramekins with the hummus, tofu spread, and ranch dressing. Arrange them on the board as shown in the photo. Swirl the hummus and tofu spreads.

2. Place the Boursin as shown and top with some of the pickled mini sweet peppers.

3. Arrange the black-eyed peas to form the ground at the bottom of the board.

4. Place the trimmed pickled asparagus and pickled carrots underneath the ramekins to look like they are growing out of the black-eyed pea "soil." Arrange the remaining asparagus and carrots as branches off the main stems.

5. Arrange the halved mini sweet peppers and endive leaves to look like petals blooming from the three ramekins. Place the broccoli florets around the Boursin to create foliage for a tree.

6. Scatter the tomatoes, olives, stuffed piquanté peppers, cornichons, Babybel cheeses, and remaining pickled mini peppers around the board.

7. Garnish with the fresh basil and edible flowers.

Taco Flower Power

Warm, soft tortillas with flavorful fillings and fixings can be a celebration all on their own. But a flower-shaped arrangement can take the serving style up a step. The middle of the flower is a cheesy rice dish. You'll get added pops of color from skewers of salami, cheese, and olives and extra touches of cucumber, pickled peppers, and cilantro.

TACOS

12 soft white corn tortillas

2 tablespoons olive oil, divided

1 pound ground beef or plant-based crumbles

1 packet taco seasoning

1½ cups Mexican shredded cheese

PINK SAUCE

½ cup sour cream

½ cup mayonnaise

2 tablespoons lime juice

1 tablespoon hot sauce (I like Tapatío)

¼ cup chunky red salsa

2 teaspoons chili lime seasoning

1 teaspoon salt

1 teaspoon pepper

PLATTER

16 slices Spanish-style chorizo

4 ounces Manchego, cubed

8 garlic-and-jalapeño-stuffed olives

12 ounces prepared Spanish rice

2 ounces shredded cheddar

1 cup fresh cilantro, trimmed, for garnish

4 ounces sweet pickled peppers

1 English cucumber, sliced into thin disks

1. Preheat the oven to 400°F.

2. To make the tacos: Using your hands or a kitchen brush, rub 1 tablespoon of the olive oil on both sides of the tortillas. Place them in a single layer on a baking sheet.

3. Heat the remaining oil in a medium pan over medium heat. Add the beef or plant-based crumbles and cook until done. Drain, then add the taco seasoning and ¼ cup of water and stir until well combined.

4. Top each tortilla with 2 tablespoons of beef and 2 to 3 tablespoons of the Mexican shredded cheese. Bake for 8 minutes.

(continued)

5. To make the pink sauce: Meanwhile, in a medium serving bowl, combine the sour cream, mayonnaise, lime juice, hot sauce, salsa, chili lime seasoning, salt, and pepper. Set aside.

6. Remove the tacos from the oven. (Do not turn off the oven.) Using a wooden spoon, fold over each tortilla. Place back in the oven for an additional 8 minutes, or until lightly browned and crispy.

7. To make the platter: Thread selections of folded chorizo, Manchego cubes, and stuffed olives on the skewers. Set aside.

8. Place the Spanish rice in a medium bowl and set in the center of the tray. Top the rice with the shredded cheese and garnish with a small portion of the cilantro.

9. Arrange the slightly cooled tacos around the rice bowl to look like petals.

10. Fill the ramekins with the sweet pickled peppers. Place one on each side of the tray.

11. Fill in the gaps between the tacos with the skewers, more Manchego cubes, and the cucumber slices.

12. Tuck in the remaining cilantro all around the edges of the tray as garnish. Serve the pink sauce on the side.

Edible Vase

Cheese appreciation meets ceramics class to create the centerpiece of this board. Once you master the perfect cheese mixture to sculpt with, it's simple to experiment with shapes. The flowers here come from watermelon, but you can stretch the concept to include any kind of fruit easily cut by cookie cutters. Make your bouquet as simple or abundant as you'd like.

8 ounces cream cheese, softened to room temperature

8 ounces goat cheese, softened to room temperature

4 ounces shredded Colby-Jack cheese

¼ cup pesto sauce (I love Kirkland at Costco)

1 cup baby arugula

1 cup microgreens

4 ounces whole pitted green Castelvetrano olives

Mini seedless watermelon, sliced

Fresh sage leaves

Rosemary flatbread crackers (I like La Panzanella Rosemary Croccantini)

1. In a food processor, combine the cream cheese, goat cheese, shredded Colby-Jack cheese, and pesto sauce until creamy and smooth.

2. Place the cheese mixture on a piece of plastic wrap, shaping it into a large flat oval. Wrap tightly and refrigerate for 30 to 60 minutes, or until firm enough to work into a form.

3. When ready, use your hands to form the mixture into the vase shape. Place it on the center of the board.

4. Arrange the arugula and microgreens around the base of the vase.

5. Put the olives in the ramekin and place on the board.

6. Cut out watermelon flowers with the cookie cutters.

7. Slide the watermelon flowers along with the sage leaves onto the bamboo skewers. Poke the skewers into the top of the vase and serve immediately with the crackers.

Home & Heart

Welcome Home	38
Board in the USA	43
Charcuterie Chalet	44
City of Cheese	48
State of the Heart	51
Hummus Love	52

Welcome *Home*

SERVES 6–8 | USES 24" SQUARE PHOTO BOARD LINED WITH PARCHMENT PAPER

You can build a gorgeous house in less than 30 minutes! It sounds like a promise for a new home-design show, but the show will be on your serving table with a grazing board. Welcome (and wow) family and friends with all the delicious details of this charming design. Feeling creative? Add your own accents to match a special home.

¼ cup spreadable herbed cheese, for paste to secure ingredients

12–24 thin breadsticks, trimmed as needed

6–8 slices pepper Jack cheese

6–8 slices provolone cheese

4 rosemary flatbread crackers (I like La Panzanella Rosemary Croccantini)

2 cups blueberries

9 pretzel squares

6–8 fresh oregano sprigs

50–60 thin pretzel sticks

8 ounces aged white cheddar, crumbled into bite-size pieces

2 scallions, trimmed

4 Persian cucumbers, sliced into disks

8–10 arugula leaves

6–8 Rainier cherries

8 slices spicy chorizo salami

2 ounces Colby-Jack cheese, cut into wedges

2 cups shell-on pistachios

12 ounces red cherries

6–8 fresh sage leaves

1. Using a bit of the spreadable cheese to secure, place breadsticks around the perimeter of the board, then use breadstick segments to create the frame of the house. Continue with breadsticks to create the outline of the front door with an awning above.

2. Trim and place the pepper Jack cheese to create bricks for the front of the house and chimney. Reserving one or two slices, trim and layer provolone slices to create the gabled roof design.

3. Fill in the doors and make a fence gate with the crackers. Securing with a dab of spreadable cheese, add blueberries for the gate handle and house doorknobs.

4. Securing with a dab of spreadable cheese, place pretzel squares as the windows. To create window box gardens, adorn the attic window with a cluster of four blueberries and garnish the lower windows with oregano sprigs.

5. Working from each side of the board, extend a fence of pretzel sticks toward the house.

6. Spread the white cheddar along the front of the house.

(continued)

7. Plant the trees by starting with a scallion trunk on each side of the house. Add cucumber slices in a round pattern to create a full display of leaves. Poke arugula sprigs into the cucumbers. To create the look of an apple tree, place Rainier cherries on top. Add oregano sprigs at the base of each tree.

8. Create a firepit by rolling three slices of the chorizo salami and placing them in a crisscross pattern in the yard. Secure with spreadable cheese, as needed.

9. Stack the remaining chorizo slices in the top right corner. Place the Colby-Jack wedges around the chorizo stack to create sun rays.

10. Fill in the background of the midsection with the pistachios. Lay a sky of blueberries and red cherries.

11. Create swirly little clouds by trimming the remaining provolone slices, rolling them into small rosettes, and tucking them into the fruit sky.

12. Place sage leaves (secured with spreadable cheese) along the eaves, above the door, and anywhere else desired.

Chorizo salami and Colby-Jack cheese can bring sunshine to any board and smiles to any gathering.

Board in the USA

SERVES 6–8 | USES 12 X 24" BOARD + 2" COOKIE CUTTER

A patriotic platter is fun for a Fourth of July picnic, but it can also celebrate a new citizen or salute a service homecoming. Anytime you want to display some red, white, and blue on your grazing table, you've now got a plan. Make it just like shown with fresh berries, sweet red licorice, gummy fish, creamy Gouda, and provolone cheese slices—some of our family's favorite snacks. Or proclaim your independence by swapping in any appropriately colored foods you prefer.

8 ounces blackberries

8 ounces raspberries

35 round wafer crackers

½ cup dried cranberries

6 provolone slices, cut in half

1 cup red gummy fish

6 ounces taco-seasoned Gouda, cubed

1 large red apple, thinly sliced and treated to a lemon bath (see tip on page 107)

24 red licorice sticks

3 provolone slices, cut into stars with the cookie cutter

1. Place the blackberries in the top left corner of the board first to anchor the entire creation.

2. Follow with the red and white ingredients, placing them in horizontal rows to create the stripes: raspberries, a portion of the crackers, dried cranberries, provolone slices, gummy fish, Gouda cubes, raspberries, apple slices, licorice sticks, and finally the remaining crackers.

3. Place the provolone stars on top of the blackberries.

If you have a bigger board and more guests to feed, go for the full thirteen stripes. Ideas for more rows: strawberries, pomegranate, Manchego cubes, white yogurt pretzels. . . . Red and white and tasty is all you need!

Charcuterie Chalet

SERVES 6–8 | USES 14 X 28" WOOD BOARD LINED WITH PARCHMENT PAPER

Construct this gorgeous getaway as a fun centerpiece for gatherings with friends and family. Or invite a group to make it together and share the memories. Once the foundation is in place, decorate it with pretty herbs, edible flowers, colorful fruits, and sweet treats. Don't get hung up on copying this design exactly. It's meant to bring inspiration, not stress! Even more fun than building the house will be devouring its delicious materials—including salami, cheese, and crackers.

Barbie Dreamhouse Cookie Kit

8 ounces whipped cream cheese, for edible "glue" and stucco

34–36 mini wheat toasts

8 pretzel squares

22–24 rosemary flatbread crackers (I like La Panzanella Rosemary Croccantini)

8–10 pretzel sticks

40 slices Italian dry salami

28 fruit-and-nut crackers

20 chocolate-covered orange gummy candy sticks

2 large strawberries

9 dried, sweetened oranges, 1 whole + 8 halved

16–18 whole green pitted olives

2 ounces microgreens

3 whole white mushrooms

1 or 2 scallions, trimmed

Edible flowers, for garnish

2 cups dry-roasted hazelnuts

20 grape and/or cherry tomatoes

Fresh cilantro sprigs, for garnish

Fresh oregano sprigs, for garnish

1. Build the basic house according to the cookie kit directions. Do not decorate it with the kit's design.

2. Spread a layer of cream cheese on the exterior walls and roof. Using the cream cheese to stick, add mini wheat toasts topped with pretzel squares wherever you would like windows. Place vertically two rosemary flatbread crackers with two pretzel sticks between as the doors. Lay down a layered salami roof.

3. Lay out the fruit-and-nut crackers to create a pathway from the front door to a patio area. Fill in rosemary flatbread crackers around the path to form the rest of the front area.

4. On the patio crackers, create and place a campfire with 12 gummy candy sticks. Create four chairs using four mini wheat toasts and four pretzel squares. (Glue the pretzel perpendicular to the toast with frosting from the cookie kit.) Set the chairs up around the fire, as shown.

5. Place a strawberry on either side of the pathway near the house. Using a bit of cream cheese or frosting, start from the strawberries and fence the cracker pathway with 14 of the dried sweetened orange halves. Create a front gate with olives (save three for step 7). Place the whole orange on the roof for a skylight.

(continued)

6. Tuck in the microgreens as grass.

7. Create the potted trees and plants by hollowing out the insides of the mushrooms. Stick a green olive inside each with the hole facing up. Poke the scallions into one olive/mushroom. Add edible flowers to garnish the others.

8. Decorate the rest of the house and fill in the yard using the remaining dried sweetened oranges, pretzel sticks, hazelnuts, tomatoes, edible flowers, and fresh herbs, with the frosting or cream cheese to help you attach.

Adding little details—like this firepit—can spark fun memories for your guests. What do your family and friends enjoy doing together? Bocce or basketball? Bird-watching or lounging by the pool? Personalize the accents if you can.

City of Cheese

SERVES 2 | USES 8 X 12" WASHINGTON STATE–SHAPED BOARD

A Seattle skyline made of cheese and meat? Yes, please! Make this cheesy cityscape or transport your board to the city in your heart by changing a few parts. There are so many iconic skylines to choose from. For a larger gathering, surprise your guests with creations honoring cities special to them. Your plan: Use three or more medium to hard cheeses (and a little patience) to create the buildings with dimension and detail. The salami adds taste, texture, and color to the board. Serve with a fruit and veggie platter and a basket of crackers.

2 or 3 smoked Gouda slices

2 or 3 pepper Jack cheese slices

2 or 3 provolone cheese slices

2 or 3 medium cheddar slices

3 or 4 Genoa salami slices

1 apple, sliced and treated to a lemon bath (see tip on page 107)

1 persimmon, sliced

Onion spiral crackers (I love these from Trader Joe's)

1. Trim the cheeses according to the shapes you want to create for your city.

2. Place the background cheese shapes first, then layer on the additional cheese details.

3. Trim and arrange the salami slices on the board.

4. Serve the apple and persimmon slices and crackers on the side.

Is there anything we can't create with cheese? Your city of cheese can stake its home on any appropriately sized board, but using a state-shaped board gives it a little something extra.

State of the Heart

All versions of this board start from the heart—heart-shaped fruit arrangements, heart-shaped cookies, heart-y pastry topped with fruit spread, and Brie baked to melty goodness. But from there, you can easily customize the vibes. Keep it straight-up in love with sweet, heartfelt messages on the cookies. Or let the display go dramatic and speak to a broken heart with sassier cookies and a knife poked into the puff pastry heart.

1½-pound Brie wheel

4 ounces red berry fruit spread

1 sheet puff pastry

2 red apples, cut into hearts of slices (see directions at right)

1 green pear, cut into hearts of slices (see directions at right)

1 red plum, quartered

2 clementines, quartered

1½ ounces honey

Water crackers

Heart-shaped cookies

Chocolate-and-nut trail mix

1. Preheat the oven to 350°F.

2. Cut the top off the Brie wheel, then cut a heart shape into the top rind with the paring knife or cookie cutter. Smear 2 tablespoons of the fruit spread on the Brie, then place the rind back on top. Bake for 10 minutes, or until the Brie is a little melty. Set aside.

3. Roll out the puff pastry, then cut it into a heart shape. Bake for 25 minutes, or until crispy and browned. Let cool slightly.

4. Smear 2 or 3 tablespoons of the fruit spread on top of the puff pastry heart. Place it in the center of the top half of the board. Place the Brie in the center of the bottom half.

5. Arrange the apples, pear, and plum on the board.

6. Add the clementines, honey, crackers, cookies, and trail mix.

Fill a board with fruit love!

To cut the apples and pear into hearts, cut around the core to create two flat halves. Lay each half flat side down and slice it vertically as thinly as you can. Avoiding the center slice, push the slices on both sides up from the bottom to create a heart shape.

Hummus Love

SERVES 12+ | USES 14 X 18¼" OVAL PLATTER

Sometimes simple love wins the day. Here's the platter you need when you want to show love without spending a lot of time prepping. The message will still warm your guests' hearts and satisfy their appetites with homemade grazing goodness. Hummus is always a good option, but a hummus heart fits especially well for an anniversary or Valentine's Day. For more color in your display, add fresh vegetables.

HUMMUS

¼ cup toasted pine nuts

1 (15-ounce) can chickpeas, drained and rinsed, with the outer shells removed

1 small shallot, finely chopped

2 cloves garlic, minced

3 tablespoons tahini

2 tablespoons freshly squeezed lemon juice

2 tablespoons artisan olive oil (I like Durant Olive Mill)

½ teaspoon ground cumin

Sea salt

Freshy ground black pepper

PLATTER

40 mini pita rounds

Garlic olive oil, for garnish

½ cup toasted pine nuts

1 small shallot, thinly sliced

Sea salt

Chopped fresh dill, for garnish

1. In a dry skillet over medium heat, toast enough pine nuts (¾ cup) for both mixing into the hummus and garnishing the platter. Toast for just 1 to 2 minutes, then set aside on a dry paper towel and sprinkle with sea salt.

2. To make the hummus: In a food processor, combine ¼ cup of the toasted pine nuts with the chickpeas, shallot, garlic, tahini, lemon juice, olive oil, cumin, salt, and pepper. Blend until smooth and creamy. If the mixture is too thick, add water, a tablespoon at a time, until you reach your desired consistency. Season to taste with more salt, pepper, and lemon juice.

3. Spread the hummus in a heart shape in the center of the platter. Make little indentations with the back of a spoon to create places for olive oil to pool and look gorgeous.

4. To make the platter: Arrange the pita all around the hummus.

5. Lightly drizzle the garlic olive oil on top of the hummus, then garnish it with the remaining pine nuts, shallots, sea salt, and dill.

SHOW BOARDS

52

The Great Outdoors

Solar System	56
Mountain of Snacks	59
Breakfast Hoot	60
Rainbow & Brie Board	63
Charcuterie Campout	64
Vegetable Patch	67

Solar System

SERVES 6–8

USES 18 X 22" BOARD LINED WITH PARCHMENT PAPER
+ 3 RAMEKINS AND STAR COOKIE CUTTER

Grazing boards can take your creativity far—even into space! This celestial snacking adventure showcases the crescent moon made with creamy, dreamy Brie, twinkling stars of pepper Jack, and shining rays of Gouda. Along the way, discover tasty treats of almonds, cashews, cheddar crackers, and more. Fresh and dried berries complete the out-of-this-world display.

2 ounces honey

2 ounces grainy yellow mustard

2 ounces ranch dressing (I love Toby's)

1-ounce jar blackberry jam

6-ounce creamy Gouda wedge, sliced into triangles

20 dried apricots (16 whole + 4 cut into quarters)

1 yellow peach, thinly sliced

1½-pound Brie wheel, cut into a crescent-moon shape

7-ounce double crème Brie wheel

8 ounces cheddar Gruyère with herbes de Provence, crumbled into bite-size pieces

6 ounces Asiago, crumbled into bite-size pieces

10–12 pitted whole Castelvetrano olives

12–14 coconut candied cashews

1 cup Marcona almonds

3 Persian cucumbers, sliced into disks

2 cups blueberries

10–12 blackberries

8 cheddar fish crackers

½ cup dried cranberries

½ cup raisins

3 slices pepper Jack cheese, cut into 6 stars using the cookie cutter

1. Fill the ramekins with the honey, mustard, and ranch dressing. Place on the board as shown in the photo. Add the jar of jam.

2. Close to the left edge of the paper, arrange the Gouda triangles as sun rays shooting into the platter. Place the whole dried apricots in a vertical line at the edge of the paper and the bases of the triangles. Layer the peach slices on top of the Gouda triangles as shown.

3. Place the Brie crescent moon in the center and the double crème Brie wheel in the bottom right corner.

4. Add the cheddar Gruyère crumbles and Asiago crumbles in two separate round piles as shown. Top the cheddar Gruyère with half of the olives and the Asiago with the candied cashews to add planet detail.

5. Create a mound of almonds in the lower left portion of the board. Top with the remaining olives.

6. Place the cucumber slices in a pile to create the last planet in the top right corner.

7. Fill in with the blueberries and blackberries around the moon and planets.

8. Place eight dried apricot quarters between the Gouda rays. Add one fish cracker to the top of each apricot quarter to resemble flames.

9. Create a ring of the remaining apricot quarters around the double crème Brie wheel.

10. Add the dried cranberries and raisins around the perimeter of the paper to fill in any gaps.

11. Place the pepper Jack cheese stars around the board.

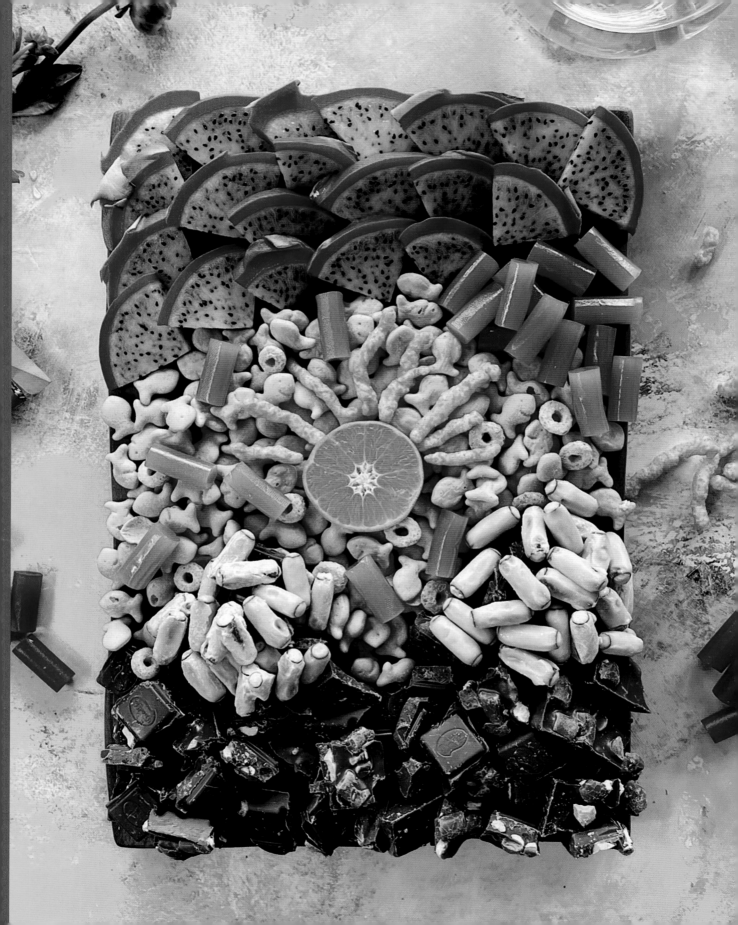

Mountain of Snacks

SERVES 12+ | USES 8 X 12" BOARD

What's better than a plate of snacks? A mountain of snacks, of course. This epic board rises to the occasion and satisfies with crunchy, cheesy, savory, sweet, and chocolaty snacks—and a touch of sunshine in the center. Swap in your favorites as you like—just follow the suggested color scheme and scale for the best results.

3 (6.4-ounce) chocolate bars (I use my favorite Darrell Lea Peanut Brittle, Caramel Craving, and Rocklea Road)

6 ounces white chocolate-covered candies (I like Darrell Lea White Chocolate Raspberry Bites)

1 cup cheddar fish crackers

1 orange, cut in half horizontally

8–10 crunchy cheese snack sticks

18–20 mango licorice pieces

10–12 orange and red fruit circle cereal

1 dragon fruit, sliced into small triangles

1. Crumble the chocolate bars into bite-size pieces and arrange them to create the mountain shape at the bottom of the board.

2. Add the white chocolate-covered candies to the peaks to look like snow.

3. Spread the cheddar fish crackers above the mountain caps.

4. Place one orange half facing up just above the mountains to look like the setting sun.

5. Add the snack sticks, mango licorice, and fruit circle cereal to fill out the orange area.

6. Arrange the dragon fruit triangles on the top area of the board.

Breakfast Hoot

Meet the cutest morning companion! Your family and friends will get a hoot from an owl with fluffy scrambled eggs for the face, golden hash browns for the body, and flaky biscuits, fruits, and vegetables for all the details that bring the owl to life. Make sure to keep the cooked elements warm and have everything else prepped ahead so you can quickly arrange and invite everyone to dig in.

1 (16-ounce) package shredded hash browns, prepared and kept warm until ready to serve

8 eggs, scrambled and kept warm until ready to serve

1 orange, cut in half + 1 thin slice taken off each half

1 kiwi, cut in half + 1 thin slice taken off each half

1 or 2 Persian cucumbers, thinly sliced lengthwise

1 slice jalapeño Havarti (I love Castello's)

1 small avocado, cut in half, with 6 small slices and 2 tiny wedges cut from one half

6 frozen or fresh biscuits, warmed and halved

8–10 fresh sage leaves

2 large fresh rosemary sprigs

2 ounces shredded cheddar

1. Set two small cups or bowls on the board in placeholder positions for the eyes. Add the hash browns below the cups and the scrambled eggs above the cups, working as quickly as possible to create the owl shape.

2. Replace the cups with the orange slices. Place a kiwi slice on top of each. Add two thin cucumber slices for eyebrows, pointing them slightly downward at the inner part of the eye.

3. Shape and place the Havarti for the nose.

4. Place the avocado wedges at the top edges of the scrambled eggs to look like ears.

5. Add the remaining cucumber slices horizontally just beneath the owl to resemble a branch.

6. Add the avocado slices to look like feet perched on the branch.

7. Place a nest of biscuits under the cucumber branch.

8. Display the remaining avocado and orange halves on the board.

9. Garnish with the fresh sage and rosemary to create feathers around the owl and greenery around the branch.

10. Serve the shredded cheddar in a cup or bowl on the side.

Rainbow & Brie Board

SERVES 2–4 | USES 9" ROUND BOARD

Just as there are certain dishes that every cook should master, there are boards that every charcuterie fan should be able to turn to. Fruit and veggie rainbows always save the day! They're scalable, customizable, relatively quick, and super colorful. No matter what the occasion, they make an impression. So start with a simpler one that calls for common ingredients, then get bigger and bolder each time. Full-table rainbow, anyone?

10 strawberries

16 raspberries

1 yellow peach, cut into bite-size pieces

6 large green grapes, sliced in half horizontally

1 Persian cucumber, sliced into disks

6 large blackberries

3-ounce Brie log, cut into 6 slices

Honey

Crackers of your choice

1. Cut the strawberries into heart shapes by simply slicing off the tops in a V-shape. Then place the strawberries and raspberries together as the first row of the arc along the top of the board.

2. Place the peaches as the next row.

3. Add a row each of grapes and cucumbers.

4. Fill the inside of the arc with the blackberries.

5. Add three slices of Brie to each end of the rainbow.

6. Serve with honey and crackers on the side.

Charcuterie Campout

SERVES 2–4 | USES 18" SQUARE BOARD + STAR COOKIE CUTTER AND I RAMEKIN

You can celebrate camping fun even when you can't get away. Pitch a tent, make a campfire, and admire a beautiful, creamy Brie moon, all on a board. There are lots of details here, but you can also add anything special to your camping experiences and memories—from marshmallows to a guitar. Don't limit your imagination! You may just need to go bigger with your board as the ideas grow.

1-pound Brie wheel, cut into a crescent-moon shape

½ cup dried cranberries

2 or 3 slices pepper Jack cheese

4 pickle slices

7 slices creamy wax Gouda, cut into thin triangles

8-ounce wedge smoked paprika Pastorale Blend cheese, sliced

18–20 whole pitted Castelvetrano olives

8 ounces aged white cheddar, crumbled

3 or 4 figs, halved

2 ounces honey

1. Place the Brie crescent moon at the top left corner of the board.

2. Scatter about half of the dried cranberries across the top of the board to create a sky background.

3. Use the cookie cutter to create four stars out of the pepper Jack cheese. Place the stars across the top of the board.

4. Slice the remaining pepper Jack cheese into little sticks to look like logs and place at the bottom of the board, as shown in the photo. Add the remaining dried cranberries just above to create the flames of a campfire. Place two pickles on either side as rocks.

5. Starting from the right top corner, run the Gouda triangles in a river pattern down the center of the board.

6. Arrange the Pastorale Blend wedge as a tree in the bottom right corner of the board. Add olives to decorate the tree.

7. Pile the cheddar near the bottom left corner as a tent.

8. Arrange the remaining olives and the figs around the board for color.

9. Add the honey to the ramekin and place on the board in the hollow of the crescent moon.

Vegetable Patch

SERVES 6–8 | USES 9" ROUND BAKING DISH

Remember that "dirt" pudding dessert we loved as kids? Here's a grown-up version of the concept, served as a much healthier appetizer of raw veggies planted in black bean-dip "dirt." Pair it with chips and a crudités platter, or expand the flavor party with a side of tacos or quesadillas. Try partnering with Taco Flower Power (page 31).

32 ounces refried black beans

1 cup shredded cheddar

4 ounces cream cheese

Juice of ½ lime

2 teaspoons garlic powder

2 teaspoons onion powder

1 teaspoon chili powder

½ teaspoon smoked paprika

1 teaspoon sea salt

2 Persian cucumbers

4 mini sweet peppers, halved

6–8 baby carrots

4 white mushrooms, sliced

1. Preheat the oven to 400°F.

2. In a medium pot, combine the refried black beans, shredded cheddar, cream cheese, lime juice, garlic powder, onion powder, chili powder, smoked paprika, and sea salt. Simmer over low heat, stirring occasionally, until creamy and smooth, about 5 minutes.

3. Spread the black bean dip in the baking dish. Bake for 20 minutes.

4. Let cool for 5 minutes before pressing the cucumbers, peppers, carrots, and mushrooms down into the dip.

5. Serve immediately with more veggies, chips, crackers, and pretzels on the side.

Spring & Summer Celebrations

Party Hoppin'	70
Charcuterie Butterfly	73
Watermelon Barbecue	77
Butter Surfboard	78
Shark-Cuterie	83
Watermelon Cake	84

Party Hoppin'

SERVES 6–8 | USES 9 X 13" BAKING PAN

Jump into spring with this adorable bunny! Two kinds of baked Brie create the bunny shape and pair perfectly with the warm focaccia bread. Fragrant herbs and olive oil take this dish to the next level. This easy, cheesy treat is guaranteed to have guests hopping to the appetizer table. You'll love it because it bakes and serves in the pan—and saves you dishwashing time and effort.

Tuscan herb extra virgin olive oil (I recommend Durant Olive Mill)

15–16 ounces refrigerated pizza dough

8-ounce Brie wheel

4.5-ounce smoky Brie wheel (try Briette)

2 orange bell peppers, tops and seeds removed

Fresh rosemary sprigs

Fresh sage leaves

Flaky sea salt

Dried Italian herbs

Rosemary honey (Naturacentric is my favorite)

1. Spread a light coating of olive oil in the baking pan. Spread the pizza dough in the baking pan. Let it rise for 60 minutes or per package directions.

2. Preheat the oven to 350°F.

3. Press down into the dough with your fingertips to make little divots. (This will give the seasonings you will be adding a place to settle.)

4. Slice the larger Brie wheel into the bunny butt, tail, and ear shapes. Use the smaller Brie wheel as the head. Press the bunny parts down into the dough in their proper positions.

5. Arrange the peppers, rosemary sprigs, and sage leaves on both sides of the bunny.

6. Top with a drizzle of olive oil plus a sprinkling of sea salt and dried herbs.

7. Bake for 30 minutes, or until the bread is browned and lightly crispy and the cheese is soft and melty. Drizzle with the honey and let the pan cool enough to handle before serving.

Charcuterie Butterfly

Spread your board-making wings by serving this beautiful butterfly at your next gathering! With three kinds of cheese, salami roses, and an array of colorful fruits, it's sure to make guests flutter with excitement. You can go bigger with the spread, as needed—just stay focused on symmetry for a pleasing display. Serve it with an abundance of crackers on the side.

8 ounces plain goat cheese

8 ounces sharp white cheddar, cut into squares

8 ounces Manchego, cut into triangles

1 large red apple

6–8 Italian dry salami slices

12 peppered salami slices

1 kiwi, cut in half horizontally

4 blackberries

8–10 blueberries

8–10 ground cherries or Rainier cherries

4 watermelon cubes

4 dried sweet oranges, halved

¼ cup Marcona almonds

3 dried apricots, 2 whole + 1 halved

2 rectangular watermelon slices

Fresh mint leaves

Fruit-and-nut crackers

2 ounces honey

1. Place the goat cheese vertically in the center of the platter to look like the body of the butterfly.

2. Fan out the cheddar slices in a circular pattern on both sides of the goat cheese to resemble the lower butterfly wings.

3. Spread the Manchego triangles in a circular pattern on both sides of the goat cheese to resemble the upper butterfly wings.

4. Slice the apple away from the core into four quarters. Slice two of the quarters thinly into apple hearts (see the tip on page 51) and place one in each center of the lower wings. Thinly slice the remaining two apple quarters, fan them out slightly, and place one in each center of the upper butterfly wings.

5. Form the Italian dry salami slices into two small roses by rolling three or four slices each (see the tip on page 143). Tuck one each between the goat cheese and apple heart on the lower wings.

6. Place the peppered salami in groups of three slices folded near the goat cheese on the upper wings and toward the edge of cheddar on the lower wings.

(continued)

7. Place a kiwi half on each side of the goat cheese on the lower wings.

8. Divide evenly between each wing the blackberries, blueberries, cherries, watermelon cubes, and dried sweet oranges. Create symmetrical arrangements.

9. Fill in the gaps with the Marcona almonds.

10. Create the antennae with the whole dried apricots, watermelon rectangles, and dried apricot halves.

11. Garnish with the fresh mint, and serve with the crackers and honey on the side.

Honey dippers add a sophisticated touch to any platter display. The grooves grab the honey and help you drizzle it beautifully rather than relying on a spoon that drips.

Watermelon Barbecue

SERVES 6–8 | USES 18" SQUARE BOARD + THICK AND REGULAR-SIZE BAMBOO SKEWERS

This is the grill everyone will want to gather around! On a rainy day or under sunny skies, the colorful spread will shine with fresh fruit and savory treats. Skewers celebrate the carefree spirit of summer and make it easy for guests to help themselves. Serving a larger crowd? Simply add more fresh skewers or even set up multiple grills, just as you would at a traditional cookout.

1 mini seedless watermelon

3 celery stalks, trimmed

6 ounces blackberries, 8–10 reserved

6–8 peach rings, cut in half

6 Persian cucumbers

6 pitted Castelvetrano olives

8–10 green grapes, sliced in half lengthwise

8–10 raspberries

6 mini sweet peppers, cut in half lengthwise

12 peppered salami slices

1. Wash the outer rind of the watermelon and pat dry with a towel. Slice the melon in half horizontally. Cut around the interior perimeter of each half with a paring knife. Make square slices into the flesh, cutting down as far as you can without cutting through the rind. Use a large spoon to remove these kebab "beef" cubes; place in a bowl and set aside.

2. To make the grill: Select one of the hollowed-out watermelon halves. Cut three slits into the rind, positioned where the celery stalks can be inserted as grill legs. Push a stalk into each slit so that the grill stands as a tripod.

3. Fill the bottom of the watermelon hollow with the 6 ounces of blackberries to look like coal.

4. Check the length of the thick bamboo skewers next to the watermelon opening. Ensure they will be long enough to go across and poke into the other side of the rind. If trims are needed, cut them with a large butcher knife. Place the five skewers to look like grates.

5. Poke the remaining thick bamboo skewer at full length through the remaining (empty) watermelon half. Connect the hollowed side to the grill by poking the skewer into the bottom on an angle (as pictured) to look like a propped-up lid. On the top edge of the skewer, attach a small piece of watermelon (or other fruit) cut into the shape of a handle or knob. Throw a steak-shaped piece of watermelon on the grill.

6. To make the skewers: Add about three watermelon cubes each to the regular-size skewers to resemble beef kebabs. Skewer the halved peach rings to look like shrimp. Skewer the cucumbers as you would hot dogs, then add an olive. For the remaining skewers, create colorful combinations of grapes, raspberries, reserved blackberries, peppers, and salami. Arrange the skewers on the board.

Get your creativity sizzling!
Use a paring knife to cut a tiny steak shape out of a small piece of watermelon.

Butter Surfboard

Hang loose and dive into a sea of whipped honey butter! You can even tell your guests you're serving octopus and then watch for their surprised reactions when they discover a crusty creature made from pizza dough. It's all good under a blueberry sky as yogurt-covered pretzel clouds float by. The scene will carry you into summer vibes any time of year.

BREAD OCTOPUS

1 pound refrigerated pizza dough

1 tablespoon salted butter, melted

1 teaspoon sea salt

HONEY BUTTER

1 pound salted butter, softened to room temperature

¼ cup honey

1 teaspoon cinnamon

1 teaspoon vanilla extract

PLATTER

2 cups blueberries

6 golden berries

1 orange bell pepper, cut into 12 thin slices

½ cup roasted tahini chickpeas

6 yogurt-covered pretzels

1 rosemary flatbread cracker (I recommend La Panzanella Rosemary Croccantini)

1 blackberry

2 blue corn tortilla chips

1. Prepare a baking sheet with aluminum foil.

2. To make the bread octopus: Divide portions from the pizza dough and roll into balls, one slightly larger than the other, for the head and body. Use the remaining dough to create eight thin strips for the legs.

3. Place the larger ball on the baking sheet with the smaller ball beneath it. Press the balls slightly together so they look like one large head/upper body of the octopus.

4. Roll the eight dough strips until they resemble octopus legs. Slightly pinch them onto the other two balls of dough, creating the full octopus shape.

5. Let the dough rise in a warm area for about 30 minutes to an hour. Cover lightly with plastic wrap to keep it from drying out.

6. Preheat the oven to 375°F.

(continued)

Do it with dough!
Don't stop at an octopus. Pizza dough makes it easy to craft tasty shapes that fit any board theme. Get creative and see what you can bake up.

7. Once the octopus has doubled in size, brush with the butter and season with the sea salt. Bake for 15 to 25 minutes, or until lightly browned.

8. To make the honey butter: In a food processor, combine the butter, honey, cinnamon, and vanilla until super creamy.

9. Cover the board with parchment paper, then spread the honey butter onto the bottom half. Create ridges to look like waves on top of the butter with a small rubber spatula.

10. To make the platter: Cover the top half of the board with the blueberries.

11. Place five golden berries in the shape of a circle in the upper right corner of the blueberry sky. Add eight pepper slices to create sun rays around the golden berries.

12. Place the roasted chickpeas across the middle of the board as the horizon line and the yogurt-covered pretzels in the sky for clouds.

13. Press the rosemary flatbread cracker into the butter to look like a surfboard.

14. Create the surfer using one blackberry for the body, one golden berry for the head, and four pepper slices for the arms and legs.

15. Add the blue corn tortilla chips in the butter as shark fins.

16. Serve the butter board with the bread octopus.

You can add sunshine to any celebration in so many ways! Gold berries and pepper slices complete the scene here. But check out pages 39, 56, and 82 for more sun creations.

Shark-Cuterie

SERVES 2–4

USES 1 5 X 25" SHARK-OUTLINE BOARD AND 25" ROUND OCEAN SCENE BOARD +
1 SMALL RAMEKIN

Cue the *Jaws* music as everyone opens their mouths to sample savory meats and cheeses with a touch of sweet and crunchy too. The shark board comes from The Hrdwood, but you can also try to create the outline on your own with just a little more patience. Using the ocean board from Backwood Design Co. adds to the ambience, but you could get creative to make your own ocean backdrop with art on parchment or a tablecloth design.

2 ounces yellow mustard

8 ounces Manchego, cut into triangles

8 ounces aged white cheddar, crumbled into bite-size pieces

8 ounces smoked cheddar, cut into squares

6 ounces salami chub, thinly sliced

6 ounces Genoa salami, thinly sliced

1 ounce dark chocolate triangles

1 ounce roasted seasoned chickpeas

14–16 seasoned pretzel sticks

20–22 oat crackers

1. Fill the ramekin with the mustard, then place it at the top of the board.

2. Arrange five Manchego triangles around the ramekin to look like sun rays.

3. Place the shark board on top of your larger ocean board to look like the shark is swimming in the sea.

4. Place the cheeses on the shark board, arranging the remaining Manchego triangles on the fins, the aged white cheddar pieces on the tail and top of head, and the smoked cheddar slices along the body.

5. Place the salami chub in a pile on the board, grouping three or four slices together near the tail, on the belly, and on the middle of the face.

6. Place the Genoa salami in a group of six slices on the belly area of the shark board and along the tail.

7. Arrange three chocolate triangles for teeth on top of the smoked cheddar slices and one roasted chickpea eye on top of the salami slices on the face of the shark.

8. Fill in the gaps on the shark board using the seasoned pretzel sticks, chocolate triangles, and roasted chickpeas.

9. Add the oat crackers along the shoreline.

Watermelon Cake

SERVES 8–10

USES 14" ROUND PLATTER + SMALL LEAF COOKIE CUTTERS AND TOOTHPICKS

This is one fruitcake your guests will request again and again! Watermelon cakes are a fresh, colorful way to celebrate so many occasions. Three slices stack beautifully on top of one another, but you can try higher if you like. Using toothpicks, you can easily add bite-size fruits, veggies, and even candies as edible cake-topper decorations. Surround the cake with even more goodies for a pleasing platter.

1 mini seedless watermelon

1 English cucumber, sliced into disks

8 ounces blueberries

2 apples, sliced and treated to a lemon bath (see tip on page 107)

12–14 dried apricots

10–12 green grapes, halved

10–12 ground cherries or Rainier cherries

3 or 4 clementines, peeled and sectioned

1 navel orange, sliced

8 ounces strawberry yogurt–covered pretzels

8–10 thin gingersnap cookies

Orange peel, for garnish

Fresh sage leaves, for garnish

1. Wash the outer rind of the watermelon, then cut it in half and slice off the rind with a sharp knife.

2. When all the rind and white matter are removed, cut three slices of watermelon from the halves. Trim the slices down, creating one large layer, one medium layer, and one small layer to stack for a three-layer cake. Set aside.

3. Cut two small slices of watermelon and use the leaf cookie cutters to create a couple of leaf details for your cake. Set aside.

4. Place the three watermelon cake layers in the center of the platter, stacking them from largest to smallest.

5. Using toothpicks, poke an assortment of cucumber slices, blueberries, apple slices, dried apricots, grape halves, and cherries into the top of the cake. Add the watermelon leaves from step 3, using toothpicks to attach.

6. Surround the cake with the remaining cucumber slices, blueberries, apple slices, dried apricots, grape halves, and cherries. Add the clementine sections, orange slices, yogurt-covered pretzels, and gingersnap cookies.

7. Tuck in the orange peel and fresh sage to garnish the platter and top of the cake.

Fall & Winter Wonders

Fall Foliage	88	Charcuterie Cornucopia	102
Football Party	93	Grazing Gobbler	107
Butter Pumpkin	94	O Tannenboard	110
Snack-o'-lantern	97	Festive Wreath	113
Spiced Pumpkin Cheese Ball	98	Boursin Tree	114
All Hands on Board	101	Caprese Ornament	117

Fall Foliage

Welcome friends and family to gather around and share in fun, food, and fall traditions. This board is perfect for fall gatherings, alongside pumpkin carving and warm apple cider. It features two delicious cheese-form flavors: Strawberry–Pinot Noir and Pumpkin Spice–Pecan. With these combinations, embracing the cozy charm of fall charcuterie is easy.

STRAWBERRY–PINOT NOIR CHEESE FORMS

8 ounces cream cheese, softened to room temperature

4 ounces goat cheese, softened to room temperature

¼ cup sliced almonds

3 tablespoons strawberry–Pinot Noir jam (I like Oregon Growers)

3 tablespoons honey

2 teaspoons dried edible lavender, divided

PUMPKIN SPICE–PECAN CHEESE FORMS

8 ounces cream cheese, softened to room temperature

4 ounces goat cheese, softened to room temperature

¼ cup chopped toasted pecans

2 tablespoons pumpkin puree

1 tablespoon hot honey

2 tablespoons pumpkin pie spice, divided

PLATTER

8–10 slices homemade or store-bought zucchini bread

8–10 fruit-and-nut crackers

4 clementines, 2 whole + 2 segmented

3 or 4 rambutan (see tip on page 90)

8 ounces golden berries

3 or 4 dried sweetened oranges

1 cup shelled pistachios

1 cup maple-bacon candied mixed nuts

Fresh basil leaves, for garnish

1 or 2 bunches red grapes

1. To make the Strawberry–Pinot Noir Cheese Forms: Combine the cream cheese, goat cheese, almonds, jam, honey, and 1 teaspoon of the lavender until smooth. Spread into three spaces in the silicone mold. Set aside

2. To make the Pumpkin Spice–Pecan Cheese Forms: Combine the cream cheese, goat cheese, pecans, pumpkin puree, hot honey, and 1 tablespoon of the pumpkin pie spice. Spread into the remaining three spaces in the silicone mold. Refrigerate the cheese forms for an hour.

(continued)

3. Remove the cheese forms from the refrigerator and place them in the center of the board. Garnish the Strawberry–Pinot Noir Cheese Forms with the remaining teaspoon of lavender and the Pumpkin Spice–Pecan Cheese Forms with the remaining tablespoon of pumpkin pie spice.

4. To make the platter: Surround the cheese forms with the zucchini bread, fruit-and-nut crackers, clementines, and rambutan. Place the golden berries near the center.

5. Fill in the gaps with the dried sweetened oranges, pistachios, and mixed nuts.

6. Garnish the board and cheese forms with the fresh basil.

7. Serve the grapes on the side.

Rambu—what?!

You can more easily find this fun tropical fruit with the spiny exterior in specialty Asian markets than in your local grocery store. It's native to Malaysia and a member of the same family as the lychee. Expect a sweet taste with a touch of tartness and a large seed in the middle, like a mango. Using a paring knife, cut into the skin to create a slit all the way around the center. Hold one end and pull the skin off the fruit.

Football Party

Score big at your next watch party with a football-shaped bread bowl! The secret to this tasty appetizer is baking the bread, artichoke dip, and cheesy topper in the oven, making everything warm and melty. Serve it with tortilla chips, veggies, beef sausages, roasted mushrooms, nuts, and salami skewers. Bet it's gone by halftime or maybe even the end of the first quarter.

1 loaf French sourdough bread

8 ounces store-bought spinach and artichoke dip (or make ahead the dip recipe featured in Green Goddess on page 124)

10–12 white button mushrooms

Olive oil

Salt and freshly ground pepper to taste

½ cup shredded cheddar

2 tablespoons dried chives

18 peppered salami slices

18–20 whole green pitted Castelvetrano olives

12 ounces smoked beef sausage, cooked and sliced into 18–20 disks

½ English cucumber, sliced into disks

2 celery stalks, trimmed into sticks

1 cup spicy candied cashews

1 cup Marcona almonds

6–8 mini whole wheat toasts

10–12 blue corn tortilla chips

Carrot fronds, for garnish

Fresh rosemary sprigs, for garnish

1. Preheat the oven to 375°F.

2. Hollow out the bread loaf by cutting off the top and then ripping out the inner part of the bread to create a bowl. Feel free to save the removed bread to bake with the bowl for dipping.

3. Fill the bread bowl with the dip and place on a baking sheet. Set aside.

4. Place the mushrooms on a baking sheet. Drizzle with olive oil and season with salt and pepper.

5. Bake the bread bowl and bread pieces (if using) and roast the mushrooms for 20 minutes. Remove from the oven and set aside the mushrooms and the bread pieces.

6. Add the shredded cheddar to the top of the bread bowl. Broil just until the cheese melts. Cool slightly, then place in the center of the board. Add the dried chives to the top to form the laces of the football.

7. Create a few skewers with folded peppered salami and olives, then place them on the board.

8. Surround the football with the remaining olives, sausage, cucumbers, celery, candied cashews, Marcona almonds, mini whole wheat toasts, roasted mushrooms, and blue corn tortilla chips.

9. Garnish with the carrot fronds and rosemary sprigs.

10. Serve with the toasted bread pieces (if using) on the side.

Butter Pumpkin

No boring bread and butter here! Gather your guests around this adorable pumpkin. A bit of tomato paste mixes with the butter to easily (and naturally) get the orange color. The cornichons and fresh mint garnish are the perfect finishing touches as the stem and leaves. Go for the great pumpkin detailed here, or try creating a pumpkin patch with several mini butter creations—just add more cornichons and mint to your shopping list.

1 pound salted butter, softened to room temperature

1 tablespoon tomato paste

Splash of pickle juice

3 cornichons

Fresh mint leaves, for garnish

Bread, warmed, or crostini, for serving

1. Whip the butter in a mixing bowl. Slowly add the tomato paste and pickle juice while continuing to whip.

2. Spread the butter in a round pumpkin shape on a ceramic platter. Add vertical lines to make ridges.

3. Place the cornichons at the top of the pumpkin to create a stem. Add mint below the stem and at the bottom of the platter to look like pumpkin leaves.

4. Serve with warmed bread or crostini.

Snack-o'-lantern

SERVES 6–8 | USES 20" ROUND BOARD + 5 SMALL RAMEKINS

Everything on your board does not need to be made from scratch—especially when you're feeding a crowd. Lean on your favorite store-bought brands to help you spend less time prepping and more time with your guests. Kids in the mix for your event? Let them help place any ingredients that aren't coming out of the oven. You'll be making memories as you make the board to share.

12–14 cheddar cheese curds, prepared and kept warm until ready to serve

12–14 packaged mozzarella sticks, prepared and kept warm until ready to serve

12–14 packaged jalapeño poppers, prepared and kept warm until ready to serve

1 cup blackberries

1 cup blueberries

1 Cara Cara navel orange, sliced

8 pumpkin-shaped sugar cookies

1 cup candy corn

3 or 4 dried sweetened oranges, halved

Ranch dressing

Bruschetta

Butternut squash marinara

Whole pitted Castelvetrano olives

Cornichons

1. Place the blackberries on the board to make two triangle eyes. Use a combination of the remaining blackberries and the blueberries to create the mouth, setting aside one blackberry for the nose.

2. Fill in the face with the cheese curds.

3. Arrange the navel orange slices around the forehead.

4. Spread the mozzarella sticks below the mouth.

5. Place the reserved blackberry as the nose.

6. Fan the jalapeño poppers and sugar cookies across the top of the board.

7. Fill in the gaps with the candy corn, dried orange slices, and any remaining navel orange slices.

8. Fill the ramekins with ranch dressing, bruschetta, butternut squash marinara, olives, and cornichons, and serve on the side.

Spiced Pumpkin Cheese Ball

SERVES 6–8 | USES 9" ROUND BOARD

In that season when pumpkins pop up everywhere, transform a cheese ball into the iconic fall shape. While you could incorporate a bit of pumpkin flavor, the flavor celebration here is simply savory—with two kinds of cheese and warm spices to create the perfect pumpkin color. The recipe goes great with your favorite crackers, fruits, or veggies. Add a touch of honey on the side.

16 ounces cream cheese, softened to room temperature

¼ cup butter

2 tablespoons pesto

2 cups shredded cheddar

½ cup chopped pistachios

1 tablespoon dried oregano

1 tablespoon dried thyme

1 tablespoon dried basil

2 tablespoons Portland Salt Co. Pork Rub

Bagel chips

4–6 fresh figs, halved

Crackers of your choice

Honey

1. In a food processor, combine the cream cheese, butter, pesto, cheddar, and pistachios until creamy and smooth.

2. Transfer the cheese to a piece of plastic wrap and form the cheese into a ball shape. Refrigerate for about 20 minutes, until firm enough to create the pumpkin shape.

3. Meanwhile, combine the dried oregano, thyme, basil, and pork rub. Spread the spice mixture on a large plate.

4. Remove the cheese ball from the refrigerator and unwrap. Roll the ball in the spice mixture until well coated.

5. Place the ball on the board. Run a straw or chopstick down the sides of the cheese ball to create the ridges of the pumpkin. Top it with part of a bagel chip to look like the pumpkin stem.

6. Serve with the bagel chips, figs, crackers, and honey.

All Hands on Board

Thrill your guests with a slice of hand! This creepy cheese-and-prosciutto appetizer is perfect for spooky season—whether you define it as Halloween or celebrate the aesthetic year-round. The hand and wrist form easily with string cheese and goat cheese. Honey pairs well for a touch of sweetness. Then wrap it all in prosciutto for a crepey skin effect. Gasp, grin, and creep it real!

6–8 string cheese sticks

8 ounces goat cheese

2 ounces hot honey, divided

7 or 8 thin slices prosciutto

2 ounces cherry or cherry Zinfandel fruit spread

Fruit-and-nut crackers

1. Trim five cheese sticks as needed to the length of the fingers and place them on the board. Slice the remaining cheese sticks and use the pieces and leftover finger pieces to help form the shape of the hand and wrist. Press the goat cheese onto the board to complete the shape of the hand and wrist.

2. Top the cheeses with a drizzle of hot honey.

3. Wrap the fingers and cover the hand and wrist with the prosciutto slices.

4. Serve with the fruit spread in a ramekin and crackers on the side.

Charcuterie Cornucopia

SERVES 4–6

USES 6 X 12" PADDLE BOARD + ALUMINUM FOIL,
PASTA CUTTER WITH SCALLOPED EDGE, AND LEAF COOKIE CUTTER

Cornucopia, meaning horn of plenty, is all about abundant beautiful foods for sharing with friends and family. And how is that different from charcuterie boards?! Let's make the marriage official by baking dough in the shape of the classic horn, and then filling it with cheese, olives, nuts, lomo Ibérico, and grapes. Your guests will be inspired and thankful.

SAGE AND SEA SALT CRACKER DOUGH

3 cups flour

3 tablespoons cold butter

8 small fresh sage leaves

2 tablespoons olive oil

2 teaspoons sea salt

PLATTER

8 ounces smoked cheddar, cut into cubes

6 lomo Ibérico slices, rolled into rosettes (see tip on page 143)

6 whole pitted green olives

1 bunch red table grapes

¼ cup shelled salt-and-pepper pistachios

2 Havarti slices, cut into leaves with the cookie cutter

Fresh basil leaves, for garnish

Rosemary flatbread crackers, for serving

1. To make the cracker dough: In a food processor, combine the flour, butter, sage leaves, olive oil, and sea salt using the lowest "dough" setting. Roll the dough into a disk shape and refrigerate for at least 30 minutes.

2. Form aluminum foil into a cornucopia shape to act as a mold for the dough.

3. Roll out the dough and cut it into 16 thin strips using the pasta cutter.

4. Preheat the oven to 375°F.

(continued)

Make the cut!
Cookie cutters can be your best friends when it comes to cutting cheese in creative shapes. Start a collection celebrating holidays and your favorite party themes. They're inexpensive tools with so many uses—from traditional cookie shaping to sandwich cutting and pancake creating. Try cutting soft fruits too.

5. Place the dough strips on top of the foil form, wrapping them all the way around and tucking them underneath to create the cornucopia. Bake for 15 to 20 minutes, or until golden brown. Let cool completely before removing the foil.

6. To make the platter: Place the cornucopia on the board and stuff it with the cheddar cubes, lomo Ibérico rosettes, and olives.

7. Add the grapes, pistachios, and Havarti leaves around the cornucopia.

8. Garnish with the fresh basil. Serve the rosemary flatbread crackers on the side.

Sage and sea salt is the dough to know! You can use it to make traditional crackers too. Preheat the oven to 350°F. Roll the dough out onto a piece of parchment paper to ⅛-inch thickness. Then use a pastry cutting tool or a sharp knife to cut them into your desired shape. Bake the crackers for 15 to 20 minutes, or until golden brown, flipping once halfway through.

Grazing Gobbler

SERVES 6–8 | USES 14 X 18" OVAL PLATTER

A turkey-shaped salad is the perfect side dish for Thanksgiving festivities. The vibrant combination of peppers, tomatoes, and arugula mixed with bold, creamy Boursin is delicious and will have your guests carving into it in seconds. Not only does this taste amazing, but it's fun to lay out the colorful ingredients to create the shape of feathers. Let (washed) little hands help you place the layers.

1 (5-ounce) Boursin Chimichurri cheese

6 cups baby arugula

2 tablespoons olive oil

2 teaspoons sea salt

1 teaspoon freshly ground black pepper

¼ cup red wine vinegar (optional)

½ cup shredded Parmesan cheese

4–6 red grape tomatoes, halved

1 red bell pepper, sliced into strips

3 carrots, peeled and cut into disks

1 Gala apple, thinly sliced and treated in a lemon bath (see tip at right)

1 yellow bell pepper, sliced into strips

4–6 yellow grape tomatoes, halved

1 cup chopped deli turkey

½ cup pickled red onions (I love Pink Wagon Foods)

8 ounces dill Havarti, cubed

4–6 green grape tomatoes, halved

1 red endive, trimmed, with leaves prepped

2 tiny cornichon slices

Fresh rosemary sprigs

1. Center the Boursin cheese at the bottom of the platter.

2. Surround the cheese with a bed of arugula that covers the platter.

3. Drizzle the olive oil over the arugula and season with the sea salt and pepper. Toss with the red wine vinegar for extra flavor (if using).

4. Pile the shredded Parmesan cheese at the base of the Boursin.

5. Branching out above the Boursin, place the "feather" rows: red grape tomatoes, red bell pepper strips, carrot disks, apple slices, yellow bell pepper strips, yellow grape tomatoes, turkey cubes topped with pickled red onions, and dill Havarti.

(continued)

Long live lemon!

One simple step can keep the crisp and flavor in your apple slices and stop the browning for hours. Add 1 tablespoon of lemon juice to 1 cup of water. Soak the apple slices for 3 to 5 minutes, then drain and rinse them. The magic comes from citric acid, which you can also find in lime juice, orange juice, and pineapple juice.

6. Tuck the green grape tomatoes into any gaps at the top and bottom.

7. Place the red endive leaves around the Boursin head of the turkey reserving one small endive piece.

8. Place the cornichon slices on the Boursin to create eyes.

9. Add the remaining endive piece to the Boursin to create a beak.

10. Place the rosemary sprigs at the bottom of the Boursin to create legs.

Tailor your turkey.
It's always an option to customize your
"feathers" to your taste preferences. Have fun
creating colorful layers with fresh ingredients!

O Tannenboard

Show your family, friends, coworkers, even Santa a little love! This happy tree features branches of creamy Brie, crisp apples, candied pecans, candies, and cookies to cover both sweet and savory cravings. It's a picture-perfect treat that comes together quickly for holiday gatherings. Feel free to get creative and add different layers or additional decorations.

4 ounces Brie, cut into 7 rectangles

5 slices red apple, treated in a lemon bath (see tip on page 107)

1 cup candied pecans

3 dipped peppermint chocolate cookies

4 ounces aged white cheddar, crumbled into bite-size pieces

12 small lime-flavored hard candies

6 red candy lips

4 seasoned pretzel sticks

10–12 mini chocolate-coated triangle candies

Fresh thyme sprigs, for garnish

Rosemary flatbread crackers (I recommend La Panzanella Rosemary Croccantini)

1. Place the Brie rectangles near the bottom of the board to start the tree shape.

2. Add the apple slices above the Brie, tapering as you work your way up to the top of the tree to create a triangle shape.

3. Add a portion of pecans followed by the cookies, cheddar, lime candies, candy lips, and finally the remaining pecans on top.

4. Place the pretzel sticks at the bottom to resemble the tree trunk.

5. Decorate with the triangle candies. Garnish with the fresh thyme.

6. Serve the crackers on the side.

Festive Wreath

SERVES 6-8 | USES 25" ROUND PADDLE BOARD + 3 SMALL RAMEKINS

Create a party-pleasing wreath filled with a merry mix of bite-size fruits, crispy munchies, flavorful spreads and cheeses, and salami ribbons with a few sweets tucked in. Touches of fresh basil and edible flowers complete the pretty picture. The shape of the board will keep guests circulating and enjoying the gift of one another's company as they grab some goodies. You can update the wreath concept with ingredients to work for any season or celebration of the year—and even add a photo or hand-lettered message in the middle.

2 ounces strawberry jam

2 ounces honey

2 ounces pumpkin spice hummus

8 ounces Manchego, cut into triangles

8 ounces aged white cheddar, crumbled into bite-size pieces

4 ounces dill Havarti, cubed

8 ounces cranberry-vanilla goat cheese, sliced into medallions using a cheese wire

8 ounces spicy soppressata salami

8 ounces Italian dry salami

4 fresh figs, sliced in half from top to bottom

18–20 blackberries

20–22 dried apricot slices

14–16 fruit-and-nut crackers

10–12 mini pumpkin spice yogurt-covered pretzels

½ cup Marcona almonds

4 chocolate pinecone candies

Fresh basil leaves, for garnish

Edible flowers, for garnish

1. Fill the ramekins with the jam, honey, and hummus. Place them on the board, spaced out, as you begin to create the circle shape.

2. Place the Manchego in four places around the board, fanning out the triangles.

3. Place the cheddar, dill Havarti, and goat cheese in small groupings around the circle.

4. Fold both kinds of salami separately into quarters and bundle them into groups of three or four slices. Tuck in the bundles near the cheeses and ramekins around the circle.

5. Place the figs, blackberries, and dried apricot slices.

6. Fill in the gaps with the crackers, yogurt-covered pretzels, almonds, and chocolate candies.

7. Garnish with the fresh basil and edible flowers.

Boursin Tree

SERVES 6–8

USES 16" ROUND BOARD + TOOTHPICKS, STAR COOKIE CUTTER, AND JAR OR RAMEKIN

Putting up and decorating a tree was never so simple! Boursin cheese is savory and delicious and pairs well with any kind of crispy cracker or chip to scoop it up. Decorate the outside with red and green veggies. Not a big cucumber fan? Try small strips of green bell pepper. Just follow the festive color scheme with any substitutions. Whatever you choose, don't forget the cheese star topper.

2 (5-ounce) Boursin Garlic & Fine Herb cheese

1 (5-ounce) Boursin Shallot & Chive cheese

2 Persian cucumbers, sliced into thin disks

20–22 red grape tomatoes

6–8 pickled mini sweet peppers

1 slice pepper Jack cheese, cut into a star with the cookie cutter

Whole pomegranate, for decoration

Bagel chips, for serving

Yogurt-covered pretzels, for serving

Cornichons, for serving

Hazelnuts, for serving

Pickled mini sweet peppers, served in a jar or ramekin

Fresh mint leaves, for garnish

1. Stack the Boursin cheese in alternating varieties on a large piece of plastic wrap. Wrap securely, then form the cheese into a small tree shape. Refrigerate the cheese tree until ready to serve.

2. Place the tree in the center of the board.

3. Press the cucumber slices into the cheese and attach the grape tomatoes to the tree with toothpicks.

4. Press the pickled peppers into the cheese to fill the gaps.

5. Place the pepper Jack cheese star on a toothpick, then press it into the top of the tree.

6. Arrange the pomegranate, bagel chips, yogurt-covered pretzels, cornichons, hazelnuts, and jar of pickled peppers around the base of the tree.

7. Garnish with the fresh mint.

Oh what fun!

Don't save the building competition for gingerbread houses. Make ahead some Boursin cheese forms, put out a variety of festively colored ingredients, and have your guests compete with tree board creations.

Caprese Ornament

Caprese salads are an entertaining favorite. The mozzarella cheese, tomatoes, basil, and balsamic dressing make the most exquisite sweet, tangy, creamy flavor combination. Now you can spread a little holiday magic with this ornament-shaped caprese grazing board. You can use any appropriately sized board, but this leaf-shaped acacia board from Left Coast Original adds a fun, festive touch.

1 cup microgreens

16 ounces mini marinated mozzarella balls (bocconcini), drained

8 cherry tomatoes, halved

6 or 7 fresh basil leaf bunches

2 large fresh rosemary sprigs

3 ounces balsamic glaze

1. Place a circular bed of microgreens in the center of the board.

2. Arrange the mozzarella balls on top of the microgreens, stacking them on top of one another as needed to create the round ball shape.

3. Decorate the ornament with the tomatoes and fresh basil.

4. Add the rosemary sprigs under the base of the ornament to give it a little foundation.

5. Serve with toothpicks and balsamic glaze on the side.

Charcuterie Characters

Magical Mermaid	120
Garden Fairy	123
Green Goddess	124
Fruit Friends	129
Leprechaun Luck	130
Guacamole Witch	133
Sugar Skull	134

Magical Mermaid

SERVES 2–4 | USES 25" ROUND BOARD + STAR AND MERMAID COOKIE CUTTERS

Whether you're hosting a beach bash, poolside party, or themed birthday, this creative food display will add a splash of fun. Colorful fruits, veggies, crackers, cheese, and almonds transform into an enchanting mermaid. Kids part of the event? Help them create a sea of magical mermaids. Once you form the body and face (the trickiest part), they can place the details. Any board can work, but the board shown from Backwood Design Co. completes the scene.

3 slices provolone cheese
20–22 strawberries, cut into hearts + tiny piece reserved for mouth
18–20 raspberries
4 Persian cucumbers, sliced into disks
2 small green grapes
6 sesame wafer crackers
28–30 Marcona almonds
24–26 blackberries
3 ounces Brie, sliced into small rounds
4 slices white cheddar, cut into stars and little mermaids using the cookie cutters

1. Trace an outline of everyone's favorite mermaid onto a piece of paper. Then place the paper on two overlapping slices of the provolone cheese. Slowly and carefully cut the cheese, following the outline, to create the mermaid shape.

2. Cut the eye and nose details from the remaining provolone cheese.

3. Place the tiny strawberry piece as the mouth.

4. Add the strawberry hearts and raspberries to the top of the mermaid and down around her arms and waist for hair that flows.

5. Create a fish scale pattern for the tail by stacking the Persian cucumbers.

6. Place the grapes as a bikini top.

7. Fill in around the mermaid with the crackers, Marcona almonds, and blackberries.

8. Decorate the board with the Brie rounds as bubbles and the cheddar shape cutouts.

Mermaid hair, don't care . . .

if your guests gobble it all up. Take a quick pic before the guests dive in! To create strawberry hearts, simply slice off the tops in a V-shape.

Garden Fairy

Looking to add some magic to your grazing event? Meet a whimsical character who comes bearing the incredibly delicious combination of creamy Brie (the face) and crusty bread (the hat) with jelly. Fresh, colorful fruits and veggies and savory salami slices fill in the rest of the board and picture, with edible flowers accenting the eyes, hair, and hat. Fairy dust optional.

1 pound refrigerated pizza dough

2 tablespoons melted butter

1½-pound Brie wheel

60 baby carrots

8 strawberries, 3 kept whole for hat detail + 2 small slivers for eyebrows

1 English cucumber, sliced into disks + 2 small slivers reserved for mouth

8 lomo Ibérico slices

Edible flowers, for garnish

3 ounces red raspberry jam

1. Preheat the oven to 375°F.

2. Roll the pizza dough into 15 balls. Place the dough balls on a baking sheet and brush with the melted butter. Bake for 20 minutes or until the rolls are golden brown. Remove from the oven and let cool for 5 minutes.

3. Place the Brie wheel in the bottom third of the board.

4. Add the rolls to the board in a triangle form above the Brie wheel to resemble a pointy hat.

5. Create the hair with the carrots.

6. Add the strawberries and cucumber, creating the face and hat details as shown.

7. Roll four lomo Ibérico slices into flowers and place in between the strawberries on the hat. Place the remaining lomo Ibérico slices at the bottom of the board to create a neck.

8. Garnish with the edible flowers.

9. Serve with the jam on the side.

Green Goddess

Design a grazing platter around the legendary Green Goddess! The classic dip mixes veggies and cheese into a divinely flavorful result. You can add a little extra fun to the offering by creating a face. Surround the goddess with the array of dippers suggested here or customize to feature your guests' favorites—anything with color and interesting texture that will hold up to a rich dip will work.

DIP

2 tablespoons butter

¼ sweet white onion, diced

1 clove garlic, minced

16 ounces frozen chopped spinach

2 cups chopped fresh kale

2 teaspoons salt

1 teaspoon white pepper

8 ounces cooked artichoke hearts, chopped into small pieces

8 ounces cream cheese, softened to room temperature

4 ounces Alfredo sauce

1 cup shredded cheddar

½ cup grated Parmesan cheese

½ cup shredded or chopped smoked Gouda

1 teaspoon garlic powder

1 teaspoon onion powder

PLATTER

1 English cucumber, sliced

1 red poblano pepper, sliced

Radicchio leaves

8 pickled asparagus spears, sliced to various lengths + 2 small pieces trimmed for the nose

8 pickled carrots, sliced into 3" sticks + 4 or 5 thin slices for eyebrows and crown

Fresh cilantro, for garnish

Fresh basil, for garnish

8 mini pickled peppers

Tortilla chips, for serving

Rosemary flatbread crackers, for serving

1. To make the dip: In an oven-safe Dutch oven over medium heat, melt the butter.

2. Add the onion and garlic and sauté until translucent and fragrant.

3. Mix in the spinach and kale and continue to cook over medium heat for 2 to 3 minutes, or until the greens have cooked down. Season with the salt and white pepper.

4. Mix in, one at a time, the artichokes, cream cheese, Alfredo sauce, cheddar, Parmesan, and Gouda. Season with the garlic powder and onion powder.

(continued)

5. Keep warm in the oven until ready to serve.

6. To make the platter: Put the dip in a shallow bowl and place in the center of the platter.

7. Create the face on the dip by adding cucumber slices topped with a red poblano pepper slice for the eyes, radicchio for the eyebrows, pickled asparagus for the nose, and a red poblano pepper bottom for the lips.

8. Use the pickled asparagus and pickled carrots to create the branches for the crown. Then poke in radicchio, fresh cilantro, fresh basil, and mini pickled peppers to fill it out.

9. Arrange tortilla chips, crackers, pickled carrots, cucumbers, pickled asparagus, and poblano pepper slices around the dip. Garnish with more fresh herbs.

Creative platters and boards give you and your guests fun and flavorful ways to dig into vegetables. You never know who you'll turn into a new veggie lover.

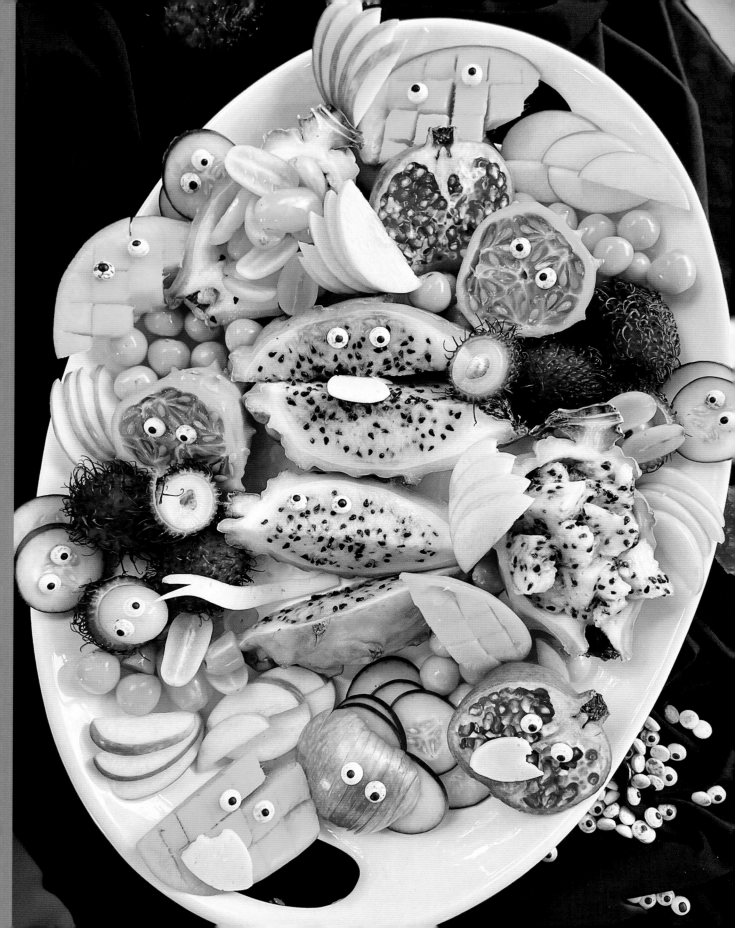

Fruit Friends

SERVES 4–6 | USES 14 X 18¼" OVAL PLATTER

Want to add a little whimsy to your gathering? Invite these fun fruit friends to your platter. It's simple to transform a colorful grouping of dragon fruits, grapes, mango, pomegranates, apples, golden berries, and the off-the-wall rambutan into a playful presentation. Have fun adding provolone details and eyeball candies—and taking in your guests' reactions!

2 dragon fruits

12 green grapes, halved

1 red mango

1 kiwano melon, halved

1 pomegranate, halved

2 small apples, sliced and treated to a lemon bath (see tip on page 107)

6 rambutans, some whole + some halved (see tip on page 90)

1 English cucumber, sliced

28–30 golden berries

1 or 2 provolone slices

28–30 hard candy eyeballs

1. Slice one dragon fruit in half. Hollow out the fruit from both sides, cube it, and then place it back in the hollow of one side. Fill the other side with some of the grape halves. Cut the remaining dragon fruit into quarters. Place the dragon fruit on the board as shown.

2. Slice around the pit of the mango, then slice the mango into quarters. Cut diagonal lines across the interior flesh of the quartered pieces, cutting down to the skin but not all the way through. Arrange on the board.

3. Place the kiwano melon halves and pomegranate halves on the board.

4. Add the apples, fanning out in groups of three or four slices.

5. Fill in the gaps with the rambutans, cucumber slices, golden berries, and remaining grapes.

6. Using a paring knife, cut out two or three mouth shapes from the provolone. Cut one longer strip into a tongue for a silly aesthetic. Add to selected fruits on the board.

7. Add the eyeballs to selected fruits on the board.

Meet a fun fruit.

Never had a kiwano melon (sometimes called a horned melon) before? You are in for a real treat. This tropical fruit comes from Africa and turns a glorious yellow-orange when it is ready to be devoured. Simply slice your fruit in half horizontally, then scoop out the inside with a spoon. So tasty!

Leprechaun Luck

SERVES 6–8 | USES 18" OVAL PLATTER LINED WITH PARCHMENT PAPER

Your lucky guests! The savory flavors in this leprechaun graze almost leap off the board. Use creamy hummus for the face; sweet, crunchy bell peppers for the hair and beard; and pickles and olives for the green outfit. Pair it with the Rainbow & Brie Board (page 63) for a spectacular St. Patrick's Day spread.

1 cup garlic hummus

1 yellow bell pepper, sliced into thin strips

10–12 blackberries

1 Persian cucumber, sliced into 12–14 thin disks with ends reserved

22–24 whole pitted green Castelvetrano olives

20–22 dill pickle slices

1 slice pepper Jack cheese, cut into a square with a center square cut out

1 red grape tomato

8 ounces Asiago, crumbled into bite-size pieces

2 cups Marcona almonds

1. Spread the hummus in the center of the platter, smoothing it and creating a round face shape.

2. Create hair and a beard with yellow pepper slices, reserving a few slices for later use.

3. Make the hat by using blackberries, cucumbers, olives, and pickles.

4. Add a buckle to the hat with the pepper Jack cheese. Then add a small yellow pepper segment to each side.

5. Create the face detail using cucumber slices for eyes, the cucumber ends for the pupils. the tomato for a nose, and more yellow pepper segments for a mouth and eyebrows.

6. Fill in around the leprechaun with the Asiago, Marcona almonds, olives, and pickles.

Guacamole Witch

SERVES 8+ | USES 18" SQUARE BOARD

Enchant your taste buds with this playful platter! Guacamole goes wild with a witchy disguise but still tastes like the creamy favorite we all love. You'll be surprised by how easy it is to come up with creative details that are also delicious. Serve the guac with blue corn tortilla chips that magically become the witch's hat. Add prosciutto for the nose and mouth, olives for the eyes, orange bell peppers for the hair, even a pea for a wart. Which part of the witch will your guests dive into first?

GUACAMOLE

10 small avocados

Juice of 2 limes

¼ cup chopped fresh cilantro

¼ sweet yellow onion, diced

Sea salt to taste

PLATTER

1 garlic-and-jalapeño-stuffed olive, halved horizontally

1 black olive, halved horizontally

1 jalapeño, cut into slices with the seeds removed

1 prosciutto slice, cut in half

2 yellow mini peppers, 1 cut into 3 triangle teeth + 1 one sliced into rings

1 fresh pea, for garnish

3 or 4 Persian cucumbers, sliced

2 orange bell peppers, sliced into thin strips + 1 top half reserved

Blue corn tortilla chips

Pretzel chips

Pretzel balls

1. To make the guacamole: Cut the avocados in half and remove the pits. Scrape out the flesh into a large bowl and mash with a fork.

2. Add the lime juice (reserving a squirt), cilantro, and onion and mash until smooth and creamy.

3. To make the platter: Transfer the guacamole to the center of the platter, shaping it into a large oval for the witch's head. Top with a squirt of lime juice and a dash of sea salt to keep the top green.

4. Start the face on the guacamole by placing a green olive half topped by a black olive half for each eye. Place half of a jalapeño slice above each for eyebrows. Twist and place one prosciutto piece for the nose and another for the parted lips. Arrange the yellow mini pepper triangles as the teeth. Style the fresh pea on the chin as a wart.

5. Place the cucumber slices below the head as a neck and shoulders.

6. Create hair from the orange bell pepper slices. Use yellow mini pepper slices as an earring.

7. Arrange the blue corn tortilla chips as the witch's hat with the bell pepper top as a flower adornment.

8. Scatter the pretzel chips and balls around the edges of the guacamole.

9. Fill in any gaps around the witch's face with the remaining jalapeño slices.

Sugar Skull

SERVES 4–6 | USES 6 X 18" GUITAR-SHAPED BOARD

You don't need to wait for Halloween to enjoy some spooky fun! Make a sugar
skull filled with all kinds of sweets and treats. You can form the shape and details
on any board, but a guitar-shaped board gives you an easy outline to follow.
The board shown is from the Dolly Parton Collection at Hobby Lobby.

14–16 marshmallows

½ cup dried unsweetened coconut strips

7 round water crackers

3 small bunches dark purple grapes

**6 slices bresaola salami, rolled into
small roses (see tip on page 143)**

**4 slices prosciutto, rolled into small roses
(see tip on page 143)**

2 gummy eyeballs + more on the side

13 spicy mango gummies

2 cashews

3 slices Italian dry salami, rolled for the lips

8 or 9 fresh rosemary sprigs

16–18 organic mini gummy worms

6–8 veggie chips in ghost and bat shapes

1. Place the marshmallows in the center of the platter to begin the face. Add the coconut strips at the top of the head and five water crackers at the jaw space.

2. Add the purple grapes and salami and prosciutto roses to the top of the head to create the crown.

3. Place two water crackers for the eyes, then top with the gummy eyeballs and two spicy mango gummies as the eyelids.

4. Place the cashews as the nose.

5. Tuck the Italian salami lip roll just above the water crackers.

6. Add three spicy mango gummies to the crown, one in the mouth, and seven down the neck to look like a spine.

7. Add rosemary sprigs to the crown and to the upper lip area for a mustache (if you like).

8. Place the gummy worms, veggie chips, gummy eyeballs, and any other goodies to share around the board.

Creative Statements Anytime

Boom Box Board	138
Trending Treat	143
Fakin' Bacon & Eggs	144
Pizza Party	147
Frappé Fun	148
Love Letter	151

Boom Box Board

SERVES 2–4 | USES 18" SQUARE BOARD

Turn up the volume on your charcuterie creativity! You'll energize any get-together—from girls' night to a decades dinner—with a boom box–shaped snack board. Don't forget to blast funky '80s jams as you fill and serve the fun, flashback display of crackers, cheese, and other treats. Add awesome props (check out the fun little soda in the upper right corner) to complete the scene.

2 large matzo crackers, 1 whole + 1 broken in half to create two rectangles

2 (8-ounce) Brie wheels

2 slices smoked Gouda

3 or 4 pepper Jack cheese slices, cut into 4 rectangles and 2 thinner rectangles

3 Babybel cheeses, plastic removed and wax left intact

3 black candy balls

1 string cheese, cut into 4 strips

2 orange-colored crispy rice treats, cut into two rectangles to resemble a cassette tape

4 sweet and spicy pickled jalapeños

2-ounce mild cheddar block cut into 2 small rectangles, 2 larger rectangles, and 4 small cubes

2 white candy balls

3 pickled mini sweet peppers

6 dry-roasted hazelnuts

3 cornichons

2 store-bought smoked salmon–cream cheese pinwheels

1 cup yogurt-covered pretzels

1 cup pepper Jack cheese crackers

10–12 sour gummy candies

1. Place the matzo crackers on the board with the large piece in the center and the two broken halves flanking it on each side.

2. Add a Brie wheel on each side where the speakers should go. Top each with a slice of smoked Gouda.

3. Place two rectangles of pepper Jack side by side at the top of the center matzo cracker. Top with the Babybel cheeses, then arrange one black candy ball on each to look like tuners.

4. Place two string cheese strips horizontally across the top center of each side matzo cracker.

5. Place one crispy rice treat in between the two Brie wheels and top with a pepper Jack rectangle. Add a thinner strip of pepper Jack to the top of the other rectangle. Place two jalapeño slices on top of the larger pepper Jack rectangle to look like the spools of a cassette tape. Make one more of these cassettes and set it aside.

6. Create the handle by placing a smaller cheddar rectangle vertically just above each inner edge of the smaller matzos. Place the longer cheddar rectangles side by side horizontally above the vertical rectangles. Adjust the pieces as needed to connect the handle. Add one white candy ball at each top corner to resemble screws.

(continued)

7. Place the cheddar cubes, pickled mini sweet peppers, hazelnuts, and cornichons for buttons, as shown in the photo.

8. Add the pinwheels as a finishing touch on the speakers.

9. Spread the yogurt-covered pretzels at the top of the board. Scatter the cheese crackers around the base. Top the crackers with the sour gummy candies.

So many buttons (and fun tastes)
to keep it authentically '80s!
Caution your guests to moonwalk,
not run, to grab their bites.

Trending Treat

SERVES 4–6

USES CARDBOARD HASHTAG OUTLINE LINED WITH PARCHMENT PAPER
+ 4 SMALL (2-OUNCE) CUPS

Good food is always trending! This easily customizable concept will elevate any occasion, whether you're sharing it with friends at a get-together or making it as a gift for someone special. Fill a letter, number, or symbol box with cured meats, artisanal cheeses, pickles, nuts, fresh and dried fruit, and herbal and floral flourishes. Or swap in candies for a sweet treat. To find outlines to purchase or make, search for "charcuterie letter boxes."

12 triangles Manchego

8 ounces Vino Rosso cheese, sliced

4 ounces blueberry-vanilla goat cheese, sliced

16 slices provolone cheese, styled into 3 or 4 roses (see below for directions)

4 ounces sweet sliced dill pickles, divided into 2 small cups

4 ounces ranch dressing, divided into 2 small cups

9 slices Italian dry salami

6–8 slices prosciutto

3 small bunches red grapes

8–10 raspberries

12 dried apricots

½ cup deluxe mixed nuts

¼ cup shell-on pistachios

Fresh sage leaves, for garnish

Fresh thyme sprigs, for garnish

Roses, for garnish

1. Create a Manchego "zipper": Take two Manchego triangles and stand them up, then flip them in opposite directions. Do this with two more sets of triangles, then push the six slices closer together. Place in the outline. Repeat to create and place another Manchego zipper.

2. Place the Vino Rosso cheese, goat cheese, and provolone roses.

3. Add the cups of pickles and ranch dressing.

4. Fold the salami into groups of three slices and tuck them into the hashtag.

5. Fold the prosciutto into groups of three or four slices and tuck them into the hashtag.

6. Add the grapes, raspberries, and dried apricots.

7. Fill in the gaps with the deluxe mixed nuts and pistachios.

8. Garnish with fresh sage, thyme, and rosebuds or petals.

Wrap a rose.

Provolone slices of about 2-inch diameter work best. (To trim a larger slice, use a circle-shaped cookie cutter.) On a large flat surface, place a few slices in a long row, layering them so that each slice is covering half of the slice before it. Roll the slices tightly from one side. You can add more slices around the outside to fill out the "petals."

CREATIVE STATEMENTS ANYTIME

143

Fakin' Bacon & Eggs

SERVES 4 | USES 12" ROUND PLATTER + 3 LARGE BAMBOO SKEWERS

Brunch just wants to have fun! Indulge in a whimsical charcuterie board that features savory salami, two kinds of cheese, and crispbreads disguised as favorite breakfast foods. It's easy to order up additional "breakfast special" plates if you're hosting a larger group. Add on traditional breakfast fruits and serve with a pot of coffee on the side for the full effect.

8 slices provolone cheese

8 medium cheddar slices, cut into small circles

12 slices soppressata salami

4 whole wheat crispbreads (I recommend Wasa)

Selection of breakfast fruits, such as clementines and bananas

1½ ounces habanero pepper jelly

Butter (optional)

1. Spread the provolone cheese slices on the platter. Top each slice with a cheddar circle to resemble an egg white and egg yolk.

2. Skewer three or four salami slices onto each bamboo skewer, ruffling them up a bit to look like bacon.

3. Arrange the crispbreads and fruit on the plate to complete the breakfast scene.

4. Serve with jelly and butter (if using) on the side.

Pizza Party

Pizza just may be the most perfect food ever made. Warm, cheesy, doughy goodness with any choice of topping sounds sublime. How about a little twist on this favorite that makes it easy to share and enjoy as an appetizer? With this pizza dip, you'll savor the flavors of pepperoni and four cheeses with each scoop. It's a slice of happiness!

8 ounces cream cheese, softened to room temperature

8 ounces plain goat cheese, softened to room temperature

½ cup grated Parmesan cheese

1 clove garlic, minced

2 teaspoons garlic powder

1 teaspoon onion powder

2 tablespoons olive oil, divided

2 teaspoons sea salt

1 pound refrigerated pizza dough

8 ounces store-bought marinara sauce

2 ounces goat cheese, crumbled

24–26 pepperoni slices + more for serving

6 slices fresh mozzarella cheese

Mini naan dippers

Pretzel chips

Rosemary flatbread crackers

1 English cucumber, sliced

1 cup shelled salt-and-vinegar pistachios

Fresh basil leaves, for garnish

1. To prepare the pizza dip: Whisk together the cream cheese and the goat cheese until creamy and smooth. Add the Parmesan, garlic, garlic powder, onion powder, and 1 tablespoon of the olive oil. Season with the sea salt. Set aside.

2. To prepare the pizza crust: Preheat the oven to 375°F.

3. Separate enough dough to make six 1-inch balls. Then roll out the remaining dough and press it into a long, flat triangle shape. Drizzle the remaining olive oil on a baking sheet and place the dough triangle on it. Arrange the dough balls along the flat top of the triangle to look like the crust on a slice of pizza. Bake for 10 to 15 minutes, or until the dough has firmed up enough to hold the creamy dip.

4. Remove the pizza slice crust from the oven. Allow it to cool on the baking sheet for about 5 minutes. (Do not turn off the oven yet.)

5. Spread the cheese mixture on the triangle. Then layer on the marinara sauce, crumbled goat cheese, pepperoni, and mozzarella. Bake for 15 to 20 minutes, or until the pizza dip is melted and bubbling.

6. Remove from the oven and let cool for 5 minutes before transferring to the platter.

7. Surround the pizza dip with naan dippers, pretzel chips, rosemary flatbread crackers, cucumber slices, pistachios, and more pepperoni slices. Garnish with fresh basil.

Frappé Fun

Bring a little coffee shop fun to your charcuterie and brighten your friends' or coworkers' day. This board may be lacking in caffeine, but not flavor or creativity! And it's simple to make, so you can even create multiple boards customized with name labels—just like the chain that writes on your cup.

1-pound Brie wheel, cut in half (reserve other half for another use)

20–22 fruit-and-nut crackers

3 ounces sharp white cheddar, sliced into squares + 1 heart shape

5 thin cucumber slices

1 fresh rosemary sprig

½ cup fig jam

Honey

1. Place the Brie wheel half with the flat side down near the top of the platter to resemble a domed lid filled with whipped cream.

2. Arrange the fruit-and-nut crackers as the "coffee" on the board, tapering the bottom slightly like the bottom of an iced-coffee cup.

3. Place the sharp cheddar slices on top of the crackers to make ice cubes.

4. Add the cucumber slices in a circle pattern on top of the cheese in the center of the cup.

5. Place the cheddar heart on top of the cucumber slices for the emblem.

6. Tuck the rosemary sprig into the top of the Brie for a straw.

7. Serve with fig jam and honey on the side.

Love Letter

SERVES 1 OR 2 | USES 14 X 18¼" OVAL PLATTER

Here's a board designed for more intimate gatherings. Show your feelings with a (literally!) cheesy love letter. The letter is made of cheese slices in the shape of an envelope and decorated with sweet and juicy sliced fruits. Make it extra lovey-dovey with apples sliced into heart shapes. Fruit and cheese are exceptionally better with drizzles of honey, so add a small jar on the side.

9 slices Havarti

2 Fuji apples

2 fresh figs, halved

6 blackberries

18–20 ground cherries

8 dried apricots

Fresh basil leaves, for garnish

Fresh sage leaves, for garnish

Honey

1. Trim the Havarti slices to create four squares, two triangles, two smaller triangles, and a tiny circle.

2. Place the squares in the center of the platter to form a larger square to resemble an envelope. Arrange the two triangles, as shown, to look like flaps. Place the two smaller triangles on top. Add the circle to the point in the middle of the cheese.

3. Slice an apple into hearts by cutting around the core to create two flat halves. Lay each half flat side down and slice it vertically as thinly as you can. Avoiding the center slice, push the slices on both sides up from the bottom to create a heart shape. Place the hearts on the platter. Slice the remaining apple traditionally and fan out the slices on the platter.

4. Scatter the figs around the platter artfully.

5. Add the blackberries in two bunches.

6. Scatter the ground cherries around the board in four bunches, spreading out the color.

7. Arrange two or three groups of dried apricots on the platter.

8. Garnish with the fresh basil and sage.

9. Serve with honey on the side.

Index

A

All Hands on Board, 101
almonds, 88
  Marcona, 56, 57, 73, 74,
    93, 113, 120, 130
apples, 43, 48, 51, 73, 84,
  107, 110, 129, 151
  cut into hearts, 14, 51
  lemon bath for, 107
apricots, dried, 24, 56, 73,
  74, 84, 113, 143, 151
arugula, 35, 38, 40, 107
Asiago, 56, 57, 130
asparagus, 28, 124, 126
avocados, 60, 133

B

Babybel cheese, 28, 138
bagel chips, 114
balsamic glaze, 117

bananas, 144
Barbie Dreamhouse
  Cookie Kit, 44, 46
basil, 27, 88, 90, 102, 104,
  113, 117, 124, 126, 147, 151
biscuits, 60
black beans, 67
blackberries, 20, 43, 56,
  57, 63, 73, 74, 77, 78, 80,
  97, 113, 120, 130, 151
blackberry jam, 56
black-eyed peas, 28
Blooming Basket, 20
blueberries, 20, 23, 38,
  40, 56, 57, 73, 74, 78,
  80, 84, 97
Board in the USA, 43
Boom Box Board, 138, 140
Boursin Chimichurri
  cheese, 107, 108
Boursin Garlic & Fine Herb
  Cheese, 114

Boursin Shallot & Chive
  cheese, 28, 114
Boursin Tree, 114
bowls, 13
breads, 94
  biscuits, 60
  French baguette, 23
  sourdough, 93
breadsticks, 38
Breakfast Hoot, 60
Brie, 51, 56, 63, 64, 70,
  110, 120, 123, 138, 148
broccoli, 28
butter, 78, 80, 94, 98, 123,
  144
Butter Pumpkin, 94
Butter Surfboard, 78, 80

C

candies
  candy balls, 138

candy corn, 97

candy lips, 110

chocolate pinecone, 113

chocolate triangle, 110

eyeball, 129

gummy, 43, 44, 134, 138, 140

lime-flavored, 110

white chocolate–covered, 59

Caprese Ornament, 117

carrot fronds, for garnish, 93

carrots, 28, 67, 107, 123, 124, 126

cashews, 56, 57, 93, 134

Castelvetrano olives, 24, 35, 56, 57, 64, 77, 93, 97, 130

celery, 77, 93

cereal, fruit circle, 59

charcuterie boards

for celebrations, 8, 11, 16

creating, 12–16

prep-ahead, 11

reactions to, 8

sharing, on social media, 16

timeline for, 16

versatility of, 11

Charcuterie Butterfly, 73

Charcuterie Campout, 64

Charcuterie Chalet, 44, 46

charcuterie characters boards

Fruit Friends, 129

Garden Fairy, 123

Green Goddess, 124, 126

Guacamole Witch, 133

Leprechaun Luck, 130

Magical Mermaid, 120

Sugar Skull, 134

Charcuterie Cornucopia, 102, 104

cheddar, 31, 32, 48, 60, 67, 93, 98, 138, 140, 144

smoked, 83, 102, 104

white, 38, 64, 73, 83, 110, 113, 120, 148

cheddar cheese curds, 97

cheddar fish crackers, 56, 57, 59

cheese knives, 13

cheeses. *See also specific cheeses*

amount, on board, 15

placement of, 13

cheese snack sticks, 59

cherries, 38, 40, 73, 74, 84, 151

chickpeas, 78, 80, 83

chives, 93

chocolate bars, 59

chocolate triangles, 83

chorizo, 31, 32

chorizo salami, 38, 40

cilantro, for garnish, 31, 32, 44, 46, 124, 126

City of Cheese, 48

clementines, 20, 27, 51, 84, 88, 90, 144

coconut strips, 134

Colby-Jack cheese, 35, 38, 40

color, importance of, 15

cookie cutters uses, 102

cookies

gingersnap, 84

heart-shaped, 51

peppermint chocolate, 110

sugar, 97

cornichons, 28, 94, 97, 107, 108, 114, 138, 140

crackers, 63, 98

cheddar fish, 56, 57, 59

fig, 27

fruit-and-nut, 44, 73, 74, 88, 90, 101, 113, 148

matzo, 138

oat, 83

onion spiral, 48

pepper Jack cheese, 138, 140

rosemary flatbread, 35, 38, 44, 78, 80, 102, 104, 110, 124, 126, 147

wafer, 43, 120

water, 51, 134

whole wheat crispbreads, 144

zucchini, 88, 90

cranberries, dried, 27, 43, 56, 57, 64

cream cheese, 23, 27, 35, 44, 67, 88, 98, 147

creative statements

anytime boards

Boom Box Board, 138, 140

Fakin' Bacon & Eggs, 144

Frappé Fun, 148

Love Letter, 151

Pizza Party, 147

Trending Treat, 143

crispbreads, 144

crispy rice treats, 138

crostini, 94

cucumbers, 148

English, 20, 31, 32, 84, 93, 123, 124, 126, 129, 147

Persian, 24, 38, 40, 56, 57, 60, 63, 67, 77, 114, 120, 130, 133

D

dill, for garnish, 52

dips

Green Goddess, 124

guacamole, 133

spinach and artichoke, 93

dishes

filling, 15

placement of, 13

dragon fruit, 59, 129

E

Eat Beautifully method, 13–15

edible flowers, for garnish, 15, 28, 44, 46, 113, 123

Edible Vase, 35

eggs, 60

endive, 28, 107, 108

F

Fakin' Bacon & Eggs, 144

Fall Foliage, 88, 90

fall & winter wonders

boards

All Hands on Board, 101

Boursin Tree, 114

Butter Pumpkin, 94

Caprese Ornament, 117

Charcuterie Cornucopia, 102, 104

Fall Foliage, 88, 90

Festive Wreath, 113

Football Party, 93

Grazing Gobbler, 107, 108

O Tannenboard, 110

Snack-o'-lantern, 97

Spiced Pumpkin Cheese Ball, 98

favor bags, 15

Festive Wreath, 113

fig crackers, 27

fig jam, 148

figs, 64, 98, 113, 151

flowers. See edible flowers, for garnish

food labels, 13

Football Party, 93

Frappé Fun, 148

French baguette, 23

fruit and floral boards

Blooming Basket, 20

Edible Vase, 35

Peachy Picnic, 27

Pineapple Perfection, 23

Sunflower Spread, 24

Taco Flower Power, 31–32

Wildflower Crudités, 28

fruit-and-nut crackers, 44, 73, 74, 88, 90, 101, 113, 148

Fruit Friends, 129

fruits. See also specific fruits

choosing, 14, 15

fancy cutting of, 14

placement of, 14

fruit spreads, 51, 101

G

Garden Fairy, 123
garlic-and-jalapeño-
    stuffed olives, 31, 32, 133
garnishes, placement of, 15
goat cheese, 23, 35, 73,
    88, 101, 147
    blueberry-vanilla, 143
    cranberry-cinnamon, 27
    cranberry-vanilla, 113
    mango-habanero, 27
golden berries, 78, 80, 88,
    90, 129
Gouda, 24, 43, 48, 56, 64,
    138
grapes
    green, 60, 77, 84, 120,
        129
    purple, 134
    red, 20, 88, 90, 102, 104,
        143
Grazing Gobbler, 107, 108
grazing table, 12
great outdoors boards
    Breakfast Hoot, 60
    Charcuterie Campout, 64
    Mountain of Snacks, 59
    Rainbow & Brie Board,
        63
    Solar System, 56–57
    Vegetable Patch, 67
Green Goddess, 124, 126

Green Goddess dip, how
    to make, 124
ground cherries, 73, 84,
    151
Gruyère, 56, 57
guacamole, how to make,
    133
Guacamole Witch, 133
guava, fancy cutting of, 14
gummy candies
    candy sticks, 44
    eyeballs, 134
    fish, 43
    sour, 138, 140
    spicy mango, 134
    worms, 134

H

habanero pepper jelly, 144
hash browns, 60
Havarti, 20, 60, 102, 104,
    107, 113, 151
hazelnuts, 44, 46, 114, 138,
    140
herbed cheese, 38
herbs, for garnish, 15.
    See also specific herbs
home and heart boards
    Board in the USA, 43
    Charcuterie Chalet, 44,
        46
    City of Cheese, 48

Hummus Love, 52
    State of the Heart, 51
    Welcome Home, 38, 40
honey, 23, 24, 27, 51, 56,
    63, 64, 70, 73, 74, 88,
    98, 101, 113, 148, 151
honey butter, 78, 80
honey dippers, 74
hummus
    balsamic, 28
    garlic, 130
    homemade, 52
    pumpkin spice, 113
Hummus Love, 52

I

ingredients
    choosing, 12, 15, 16
    order of placement for,
        13–15
    preparing, 12–13

J

jalapeño poppers, 97
jalapeños, 133, 138
jalapeño tofu spread, 28
jam
    blackberry, 56
    fig, 148
    raspberry, 123
    strawberry, 113
    strawberry–Pinot Noir, 88

K

kiwano melon (horned melon), 129
kiwi, 60, 73, 74
  fancy cutting of, 14
knives, cheese, 13

L

lavender, 88
lemon bath, for preserving apples, 107
lemons, 20
Leprechaun Luck, 130
licorice, 43, 59
limes, 20, 67
lomo Ibérico, 102, 104, 123
Love Letter, 151

M

Magical Mermaid, 120
Manchego, 20, 27, 31, 32, 73, 83, 113, 143
mango, 129
  scoring, 14
mango gummies, 134
maple-bacon mixed nuts, 88, 90
Marcona almonds, 56, 57, 73, 74, 93, 113, 120, 130
marinara sauce, 147
marshmallows, 134

matzo crackers, 138
meats
  placement of, 14
  styling, 14
microgreens, 35, 44, 46, 117
mini wheat toasts, 44, 93
mint, for garnish, 73, 74, 94, 114
Mountain of Snacks, 59
mozzarella, 97, 117, 147
mushrooms, 44, 46, 67, 93
music, for parties, 15
mustard, 24, 56, 83

N

naan dippers, 147
napkins, 13
nuts. See also specific nuts
  mixed, 143

O

oat crackers, 83
olive oil, 147
  for garnish, 52
  Tuscan herb, 70
olives
  black, 133
  Castelvetrano, 24, 35, 56, 57, 64, 77, 93, 97, 130
  garlic-and-jalapeño-stuffed, 31, 32, 133
  green, 28, 44, 102, 104

onions, pickled, 107
onion spiral crackers, 48
oranges, 59, 60, 84, 97
  dried, 44, 73, 74, 88, 90
oregano sprigs, 20, 38, 40, 44, 46
O Tannenboard, 110

P

pantry items, placement of, 14–15
parchment paper, 13
Parmesan cheese, 107, 147
parsley sprigs, 24
Party Hoppin', 70
party planning, 11–12
party playlist, 15
Pastorale Blend cheese, 64
peaches, 23, 24, 27, 56, 63
  grilling, 27
peach rings, 77
Peachy Picnic, 27
pears, 51
  cut into hearts, 14, 51
pecans, 23, 88, 110
pepper Jack cheese, 38, 48, 56, 57, 64, 114, 130, 138
pepper Jack cheese crackers, 138, 140
pepperoni, 147

peppers
  bell, 70, 78, 80, 107, 130, 133
  jalapeño, 133, 138
  mini sweet, 28, 67, 77, 114, 138, 140
  pickled, 114, 124, 126
  piquanté, 28
  poblano, 124, 126
  sweet pickled, 31, 32, 114
persimmon, 48
pesto sauce, 35, 98
pickles, 64, 130, 143
pineapple, pineapple juice, 23
Pineapple Perfection, 23
pine nuts, 52
pink sauce, 31, 32
pistachios, 38, 40, 88, 90, 98, 102, 104, 143, 147
pita rounds, 52
pizza dough, 70, 78, 123, 147
  for crafting shapes, 78
Pizza Party, 147
plates, small, 13
platters and boards
  accessories for, 13
  arranging ingredients on, 13–15
  choosing, 12
playlist, for parties, 15
plums, 51

pomegranate, 114, 129
Portland Salt Co. Pork Rub, 98
pretzels, 38, 44, 83, 110, 133, 147
  yogurt-covered, 78, 80, 84, 113, 114, 138, 140
produce. See fruits; vegetables
prosciutto, 101, 134, 143
provolone, 38, 40, 43, 48, 120, 129, 143, 144
provolone roses, 143
puff pastry, 51
pumpkin puree, 88
Pumpkin Spice–Pecan Cheese Forms, 88, 90

R

radicchio, 124, 126
Rainbow & Brie Board, 63
Rainier cherries, 38, 40, 73, 84
raisins, 24, 56, 57
rambutans, 88, 90, 129
  cutting, 90
ramekins, 13
ranch dressing, 28, 56, 97, 143
raspberries, 43, 63, 77, 120, 143
raspberry jam, 123

refried black beans, 67
rosemary flatbread
  crackers, 35, 38, 44, 78, 80, 102, 104, 110, 124, 126, 147
rosemary sprigs, 60, 70, 93, 107, 117, 134, 148
roses, for garnish, 143
roses, provolone, 143

S

Sage and Sea Salt Cracker Dough, 102, 104
sage leaves, 35, 38, 40, 60, 70, 84, 102, 143, 151
salami, 83
  bresaola, 134
  Genoa, 48, 83
  Italian dry, 20, 44, 73, 113, 134, 143
  peppered, 73, 77, 93
  soppressata, 113, 144
sausage, beef, 93
scallions, 38, 40, 44, 46
serving tools, 13
shallots, 52
Shark-Cuterie, 83
small plates, 13
smoked salmon–cream cheese pinwheels, 138, 140
Snack-o'-lantern, 97

Solar System, 56–57
Spanish rice, 31, 32
Spiced Pumpkin Cheese
  Ball, 98
spinach and artichoke dip,
  93
spoons, 13
spring & summer
  celebrations boards
  Butter Surfboard, 78, 80
  Charcuterie Butterfly,
    73–74
  Party Hoppin', 70
  Shark-Cuterie, 83
  Watermelon Barbecue, 77
  Watermelon Cake, 84
State of the Heart, 51
state-shaped boards, 48
strawberries, 20, 27, 44,
  63, 120, 123
  cut into hearts, 14, 120
strawberry jam, 113
Strawberry–Pinot Noir
  Cheese Forms, 88, 90
strawberry–Pinot Noir jam,
  88
string cheese, 101, 138
Sugar Skull, 134
Sunflower Spread, 24
sunshine creations, 80

T

Taco Flower Power, 31–32
tacos, 31, 32
Thai basil, for garnish, 28
thyme sprigs, for garnish,
  110, 143
tofu spread, jalapeño, 28
tomatoes
  cherry, 28, 44, 46, 117
  grape, 107, 108, 114, 130
tongs, 13
tortilla chips, 78, 80, 93,
  124, 126, 133
tortillas, 31
trail mix, 51
Trending Treat, 143
turkey, deli, 107
tzatziki, 24

V

Vegetable Patch, 67
vegetables. *See also*
  specific vegetables
  choosing, 14, 15
  placement of, 14
veggie chips, 134
Vino Rosso cheese, 143

W

wafer crackers, 43, 120
walnuts, 27
water crackers, 51, 134
watermelon, 35, 73, 74,
  77, 84
Watermelon Barbecue, 77
Watermelon Cake, 84
Welcome Home, 38, 40
whole wheat crispbreads,
  144
Wildflower Crudités, 28

Y

yogurt-covered pretzels,
  78, 80, 84, 113, 114, 138,
  140

Z

zucchini bread, 88, 90